From RUIN to RESTORATION

Steps to Rekindle a Broken Marriage

Kay Cherry

Scripture quotations are from:

King James Version, Published by The World Publishing Company, Cleveland, Ohio

The Living Bible, copyright 1971 Tyndale House Publishers, Wheaton, IL

New American Standard Bible, copyright 1979 Published by Thomas Nelson Publishers

Nashville · Camden · New York

The Amplified Bible

The New Living Translation Bible

7710-T Cherry Park Dr, Ste 224
Houston, TX 77095
(713) 766-4271

Printed in the United States of America

ISBN: 978-1-68411-869-4

Dedication

To my husband of more than four decades, Ron, who is my champion – a man passionately devoted to his family and to whom I am profoundly grateful for centering our family on the foundation of God's Word.

To our son, Jason and his wife Ginny, and our daughter, Ashley and her husband, Steven Smith, who have faithfully provided healthy homes and role models for our grandchildren to follow.

To my friends who encouraged me to write our story.

To my readers for whom I've written this story. As you apply the principles that rekindled our love relationship to your own marriage, may you experience peace and contentment, and, may your life, in turn, become a testimony to the world and future generations of the restorative power of Almighty God.

Special thanks to Eddie Smith who allowed this project to come to life and helped us complete the book after Kay's passing.

Foreword

When I first met Kay Cherry, I was dating her daughter and determined to impress her. To my delight she was so engaging. She laughed at my jokes, looked me in the eye, and gave me compliments. So, you can imagine how disappointed I was to learn that she treated everyone that way! Seriously, everyone she encountered felt this grace. She treated the people of each social class the same and assumed the best of everyone. And honestly, in this way she was profoundly naïve.

While naïve in the ways of the world, she had a pristine insight into people, especially the hurting. Her ability to read a room and read a situation was uncanny. She would identify the hurting person, astutely get to the heart of the problem, and meet that need. She was a counselor. She was an encourager. She was a cheerleader. While she was the last one to arrive, she was also the last one to leave. It was all about the people.

Yet, all this good was tested through trial. This is what makes her and Ron, her husband of 48 years, so amazing. They walked through the fire and kept walking. Many people, enduring far less than they, would have given up. They are both a testimony to fortitude. In the end Kay was a survivor. She survived marital, financial, physical, and family crises. She was gutsy and gorgeous. True grit in leopard heels.

As a people person, she would always choose a person over a book. She would certainly choose people over writing a book! What you hold in your hand is not an expression of someone who wanted to write, but someone who had you in mind. The joy was in communicating. Kay felt that all the very good and very bad she experienced had a purpose; it was to encourage others. As a generous soul she poured out grace to everyone she met.

In the summer of 2019 Kay went to her heavenly reward. The words appearing on my screen hardly seem real. She was so kind, generous, forgiving, and gracious toward me. My last texts from her were affectionate and warm.

In these pages her irrepressible spirit still speaks, still encourages, and still loves. Read and know she would have loved to sit down with you and encourage you to keep fighting for what was right. She would tell you to endure until what is ruined is rekindled and restored.

--Steven Smith

Contents

Introduction

My fairy tale, charmed life came to ruin. Circumstances looked bleak. I couldn't see then that God had a triumphant plan for my future, just ahead.

I remember as a little girl running to daddy to fix my broken toys. I quickly learned they were not ruined—Daddy could always find a way to restore them. It's the same for you today. God the Father can always find a way to fix the utterly impossible situations in your life when you entrust them to Him.

We hear so much today about broken marriages that it has become an expected, acceptable state of being. But broken marriages often produce broken children and ruined lives that continue to suffer pain and can sometimes struggle for generations. There can come a point where only three choices remain. They are…

- Get a divorce,

- Stay in the marriage without making efforts to improve it, or

- Work on building a satisfying, intimate love relationship.

One path leads to the defeat of divorce, another to daily misery, and the third to rich blessings. None of these choices are easy, so choose wisely.

Through the ages, couples have experienced common problems in relationships. If you want to make a case for getting out, you can always find a reason. If you do, you'll likely live with regrets, and you'll miss the best part. The most profound satisfaction comes from working through difficult situations and winning! Triumph only comes through trials. You ultimately get what you were seeking and much more.

God has a wonderful plan for your marriage. He can give you hope, rekindle your love, and restore your broken relationships. He is a master at taking the blackened ashes and cooled coals of your life and fanning the fire to rekindle love and bring back the lost warmth and intimacy.

In the dark places of life, we all tend to stumble into the same pitfalls that cause fearful doubts to plague our minds. But to those doubts, I say, "Yes, you can love again, you have value, you can still have purpose in life and be useful. And yes, you can be happy again! There most certainly is life after a crisis, so don't give up!"

Your crisis doesn't have to define you. *How you respond to your crisis is what defines you.*

If you are reading this book, then most probably, you or someone you know is in a troubled relationship. You don't have to settle for a painful or mediocre love life. You can experience a new sense of excitement and challenge by allowing the truths and testimony in this book to transform your marriage. You can begin today to make the most valuable part of your life, your personal relationship, more than you ever dreamed it could be.

Be encouraged as you read my story. Realize that you are not alone in your pain. I understand it, as do many others. It doesn't have to last. Let it go and walk in renewed faith that God can heal your ruined, broken life. His forgiving grace makes it possible to start over again. No, it won't be the same, it will be better!

If you are contemplating divorce, let my testimony of a transformed marriage give you the courage to keep trying. The consequences of quitting are too grave. God can either change your circumstances or give you the grace to live in peace in your struggles.

If you are already divorced, don't live under condemnation, accept God's love. Ask Him to restore the ruins of your life and bring you to a new place of contentment and joy.

If your marriage is healthy, my prayer is that the "Marriage Builders" herein will serve to strengthen it further and that you will pass this book along to someone you know who needs hope.

I have written *From Ruin to Restoration* because I have a passion for bringing hope and wholeness to broken people, for offering courage to those in the struggle, and for improving already good marriages.

I have written this book to remind you, as Corrie Ten Boom said, "There is no situation so impossible that God is not greater still." Not my situation, or yours!

--Kay McCormick Cherry

Part One

Our Story

Chapter One

The Romance

Born in Texas into a stable, loving, Christian family and married to the man of my dreams, my life was a virtual fairy tale.

My first recollection of my husband was when I was a fifth grader, and he was a cute, towheaded sixth grader... an "upperclassman." I remember in junior high when he starred in the school plays and won most of the speech contests for our school. Then, I remember when we served together as officers of our student body in high school. I was a cheerleader and he a football player. It was a great time of life for both of us, full and rich with anticipation of exciting futures.

Our first date was his senior prom! I proudly appeared on his arm in my gorgeous royal blue ball gown, with shiny braces on my teeth... he didn't seem to mind! We had an absolutely enchanted evening going from one event to another with our mutual friends. I felt like Cinderella when she fell in love with her charming prince. Ron was the perfect gentleman. When he brought me home that evening, I remember watching as he drove away and hoping that would be the first of many dates. I didn't want to take my dress off for fear it would break the spell. That night began our five years of dating through college and graduate school.

He was a year ahead of me in high school, so he went off to college first, four hours away. We lost contact with each other at that point. He came back home for Christmas and called me to go out on New Year's. I was so surprised! Up until then, I had presumed the distance between us would prevent our seeing each other anymore. But, that semester, we spent lots of fun weekends together, and before summer came, we had fallen in love.

When it was time for me to go to college, there was no doubt where I wanted to go. He still says I followed him there! And I guess I did. Our relationship deepened that school year, and we began to talk about a future together.

The next year, I was invited to tour the country with a Christian singing group. With my parents' blessings, I dropped out of college for a year to travel and sing, and it proved to be an incredible experience for me. There were 25 of us in the group - five girls and five guys singing, a ten-member band, our director, road manager, and sound crew. We hit the road after six weeks of rehearsal to begin an exciting adventure singing and sharing the gospel in churches and schools in every state and up into Canada. Our group was also invited to sing at a Billy Graham crusade and to do some TV spots. It was a sensational year, and my walk with the Lord deepened.

The tour took me away from Ron, and of course, I missed him very much. He drove to see me in concert whenever he could, and I looked forward to his letters with great anticipation.

Toward the end of my tour, a concert was scheduled in my hometown. I was thrilled to see my family and beyond excited to see the man I loved! While there, we shopped for the perfect diamond ring! To my surprise, in the jewelry store window was the ring I still wear with pride today. Poor Ron. He had eaten beans for an entire year to buy me the most beautiful diamond ring he could afford.

We raced back to the house because I only had a couple of hours to prepare for the concert. When we got home, Ron opened the small, black velvet box containing my ring. He nervously took my hand and told me he wanted to spend the rest of his life with me. He asked me to marry him! And, of course, I said YES! YES! YES! He put the ring on my finger and sealed our engagement with a kiss! He had wanted to do more to make the moment special, but my pressing schedule made it impossible. I bounced into the house to show my family my beautiful engagement ring and could hardly wait to wear it on stage that night! It all seemed like a dream.

When the tour was over, I returned to college, and Ron and I began spending more time together. As we did, I started having second thoughts about our relationship. I saw little "red flags" of warning that something wasn't quite right. There were many differences in how we were raised. I was from a huge, affectionate family, who loved to have lots of people in our home. He, on the other hand, was a very private person raised in a family who seldom entertained. I was having trouble imagining setting up a home where friends and family were not a valued part and one that would provide a haven for our core family and a ministry to others. This was contrary to Ron's desires.

As we continued discussing our expectations for the future, we saw other differences that made it hard to do life together. Ron is a bottom line, get-the-job-done kind of guy. His direct, aggressive nature enables him to be a man of accomplishment. I, on the other hand, am compassionate, sensitive, empathetic, and people oriented. We viewed the world from different perspectives, and if we were going to make a life together, we would have to learn how to blend our differences.

It is God's design that we complement each other by bringing into our relationship our differing strengths. We see this so clearly in the game of sports, but Satan's clever deceptions keep us from easily seeing it in the game of life. No football team could be successful with only outstanding quarterbacks. The strengths of the linemen, and guards and other team members are also essential to a championship team. Ron and I realized we would have to learn to appreciate and utilize these differences if we were going to make a life together.

We also had different communication styles. Ron, for example, prefers to have little discussion, make quick apologies, and to move on. I, on the other hand, see value in seeking to understand root causes and working together to clear them up so that they don't keep coming up.

Ultimately, our romance began unraveling as these unsettling differences continued to loom over us. I desperately wanted to be with Ron, but I was starting to believe that we were just too opposite to make this work. There were many qualities in him I admired, as did others. Young people and adults alike recognized him as a disciplined young man with a brilliant mind and a bright future.

As time went on, it was becoming more apparent that our engagement needed to be called off, or at the very least, postponed, until we could find a way to appreciate our differences. If we could do that, we could be a powerful team.

I didn't completely understand the uneasy feelings rumbling inside me, but I knew I was in anguish over the decision to break our engagement. My head was telling me to do it, but my heart was telling me otherwise. I eventually listened to my head and broke our engagement.

A year went by with absolutely no contact whatsoever. Then, we unexpectedly ran into each other face to face. My heart was racing! Coincidence? I think not! I believe it was a part of God's plan. It was an awkward moment for both of us, neither knowing what to do or say. We managed to come up with some small talk, and by the end of the brief and stumbling conversation, he invited me to come to hear him speak that evening.

My mother and aunt accompanied me as was proper for a young southern lady in those days. They strategically placed me on the aisle seat, giving Ron easy access to talk with me. Their little plan worked! At the end of the service, he briskly passed by on his way from the platform to greet guests and asked if he could take me home. During the next month, we spent as much time together as we could. It was obvious our love had not diminished in any way, and we laughed during those weeks more than we had the entire year. It seemed his character had only strengthened. Being in his confident presence made me feel secure.

We saw each other as often as possible. By the end of the month, we were engaged, and I was thrilled to have my ring back on my finger! This time, he was able to present it to me over a lovely candlelight dinner - a bit more of a romantic setting than the first time! Four months later we walked the aisle in a storybook winter wedding. I thought Ron was so handsome in his tuxedo with his "Elvis-style" sideburns, and I in my size six leopard "going-away" shoes, were to die for! I had one year left in college, and he was one year away from beginning his doctoral studies.

As students, we had little money for a honeymoon. When a friend heard of our plight, she graciously offered her beautiful, snow-covered mountain home that we thoroughly enjoyed for a week. On the way home, Ron had the opportunity to exercise great patience as a new husband due to my pitiful map skills which caused us to drive hours out of the way. We finally made it home and started our life together.

We were so happy and didn't care that we only had a tiny, two-room apartment. We were in love, and that was all that mattered.

As young lovers, we couldn't have imagined the devastation that would subtly and stealthily sneak into our romance, stealing all that we held dear.

Chapter Two

The Ruin

T he married bliss everybody talks about didn't last long. Those little "red flags" that had bothered me before marriage became more pronounced in day-to-day living than when we were dating.

In the early years of our marriage, Ron focused on being a student and pastor. My primary focus was on building a Christ-centered marriage that would bring joy into our lives and be an example of a biblically-based relationship others could follow. I admired Ron's dedication to pastoring and longed to see that same passion directed toward our marriage. Ron and I were both doing our best to be good mates to one another. We just weren't connecting.

It's God's design that the heart of a wife is her home and family. While the biblical blueprint for a husband is to provide for and protect the family and home, both husband and wife are to work on developing the marriage relationship so they can, together, center the home solidly on being a place where hearts are nourished and formed. The different roles are to be worked out daily in such a way as to bring the family together, rather than divide it.

Most couples don't realize that marriage is something to be built and maintained. It involves much more than getting a license and walking down an aisle. Nicholas Kirsch, Ph.D., a "couples therapist" in Bethesda, Maryland, says, "Know that love's not enough. Perhaps the most important lesson relationship research has taught us is that marriage, like any other commitment, takes a conscious effort to preserve." He goes on to say "So many people do lifelong training in so many things - if you're a golf enthusiast, you go to the driving range a couple of times a week. If you're a lawyer, you take continuing education. If you're an artist, you take workshops. And somehow, there's this belief that we don't have to work at learning how to be a couple, it should just come naturally," he says. "That, to me, is just very backward."

Ron was comfortable meeting the more tangible needs that required a quick and decisive solution, such as the financial ones. He felt competent in this arena. But when it came time to interact at home, he didn't know where to start, and on top of that, he was spent. He had already used up his creative juices in the long hours at work. He just wanted to relax and escape into whatever was on TV, which ultimately became an enemy to our family causing estrangement and isolation. In his exhausted state, Ron left the "marriage thing" up to me to figure out and set his mind on being a good provider, something he knew how to do very well.

One person cannot be responsible for the emotional needs of both parties in any relationship. Both husband and wife must participate to achieve a satisfying relationship. As time went on, I felt more and more alone in our relationship.

The wall between us seemed to get wider and taller over the years. Oh, on the surface, everything looked fine, and we did have some pleasant times. However, daily life was hard. Getting his cooperation on the smallest things was difficult. Most of my requests or conversations were met with resistance, and I found I was often defending my position or explaining why it was logical or reasonable. It was exhausting, and my stomach stayed in knots. It just didn't make sense. I loved him and desired to make him happy. I just couldn't. No matter what I did, it wasn't right. I felt estranged and left out of his world.

Many changes occurred in our lives during the first twelve years of marriage in the areas of education, infertility, health, the addition of children, eight moves, the unraveling of our marriage, and challenges to our faith. Some psychologists say the first ten to twelve years are typically the toughest because new dynamics and experiences are introduced into the relationship that the couple is not prepared for or inexperienced at handling.

We finally moved from student status to graduates. I earned my college degree and Ron his doctorate. It was satisfying to achieve our educational goals, but health problems became a challenge, both physically and financially. Within the first year of our marriage, I was diagnosed with a disease that caused acute pain, and both of us were disappointed that this disease marred our most intimate times.

Two and a half years later, it progressed to the point where I had to have emergency surgery. I remember waking up and hearing the doctor say, "We took out as much of the disease as we could. We decided not to do a complete hysterectomy, at this time, since you're young and haven't had children. Though it's doubtful you will be able to have a baby, we wanted to, at the very least, give you a chance."

This announcement was completely unexpected! I thought the doctors were merely removing a tumor. My lifelong dream of being a mother was being threatened, and I was shaken. I desperately needed Ron's support, his empathy, and his assurance, but he appeared untouched by the news. He later told me he was just trying to be strong for me. But at that moment, his lack of emotion appeared as cold indifference to my grief. It devastated me as much as the news itself. Once again, we were not able to communicate to each other what we needed.

We managed to get through this difficult time and began working closely with infertility specialists. To our doctor's surprise, we finally had a baby! The doctor called it a miracle, and we believed it was, too. Our hearts were brimming with joy.

When our son was born, Ron was on a preaching tour overseas. Our little bundle arrived early. A preemie. He was so fragile.

I called to let Ron know he had become a father. Seven days went by before I heard from Ron. I felt unimportant to him and embarrassed that I had no answers to the constant questions regarding his return. By the time he walked into my hospital room a week later, I didn't care if he came at all. Again, just like with my surgery, his silence was deafening, and his stoicism came across as insensitivity instead of strength that I could lean on. He presumed I would know the additional costs for overseas calls and breaking from the group to return home early would be extremely expensive. We have both since learned that presumptions can be killers to a relationship. Don't assume your mate knows what you're thinking – they probably don't!

We had to lay our feelings aside and concentrate on our baby, who was hovering at death's door. The next year, we found ourselves at the hospital more than at home. We were both physically and emotionally drained from so many brushes with near-death. I continued to experience poor health, which made it harder to deal with all the trauma. I eventually had to have multiple surgeries, and each of them, in their own way, added more stress and strain.

Our daughter's birth was a delightful surprise, arriving eighteen months after our first child. Another miracle, and thankfully a healthy one! Our little family was growing, and so was Ron's career. With such a full schedule, Ron and I spent little time together and began to drift apart. I was lonely for his companionship and yearned for a deep, intimate relationship with him.

We moved across the country where Ron took a new pastorate. Life was somewhat simpler there, at least for a while. But soon, the demands of work responsibilities increased, health issues continued, and medical bills mounted. In addition to the responsibility Ron felt toward our growing family, he felt an even deeper responsibility to God's calling on his life. This was a gnawing conflict.

As teenagers, we had both surrendered our lives to full-time ministry. We seemed to be traveling toward the same destination, but on different roads. Ron lived in his world ministering to our congregation, studying and preaching. I lived in my world, raising the children, speaking to Christian women's groups, and being involved in children's ministry. Our communication was brief, at best – mostly speaking of schedules and events, seldom of dreams and goals and the things that brought us together in the first place. Even though we had gone through so much together, I still did not feel we were of one spirit. He did. A cold distancing crept between us.

Isaiah 53:6 says, "All of us like sheep have gone astray, each of us has turned to his own way." When a couple begins to live independently of each other, it's a pathway to destruction and should be perceived as a dangerous enemy of the relationship.

The children were growing up fast and they, as well as I, needed Ron's focus and leadership in our home. He possessed many qualities I admired and wanted the children to benefit from. I certainly didn't want his neglect to breed seeds of rebellion when they grew older. He had so much to offer them, but he was independent and didn't appear to need us. I tried to slough off the rejection I was beginning to feel, but rejection is a saboteur, not to be tolerated in a healthy marriage. Nothing I said or did reached his heart or turned his attention toward us.

Though Ron sees now that God is to be first, then family, then church/career, at that time, he understood the church and God to be the same. With this mindset, it was nearly impossible to properly prioritize his time between God, ministry, and family. He felt guilty of not putting God first if he was home and frustrated at home because he believed he needed to be serving God and the church. He consoled himself with the belief that men show their love and loyalty to their family by financially providing for them and that he did well, but there was no time for building relationships at home. The conflict within him was constant. This is a common conflict among ministers.

Under Ron's skillful leadership, the church flourished, but the pressure mounted as the demands on his time increased. He eventually became so exhausted that he talked of leaving the ministry. I knew he was discouraged, but I couldn't, in my wildest imagination, believe he would actually do it. This man that had made tremendous sacrifices, for years, to prepare himself for this very time could not possibly entertain such a thing.

Not understanding all the reasons why, but sensing a great struggle within him, I purposed to pray for him in a more disciplined fashion than ever before. Neither of us realized at the time that we were under spiritual attack purposed to destroy our ministry, our marriage, and our family — a raging warfare. I responded to prompting from God to pray for Ron and our family.

I earnestly and explicitly prayed for him for a year but saw no improvement. In fact, things got worse. When this happens, we sometimes think that God isn't answering our prayers. But He *always* does. Sometimes we must *wait* for God's perfect timing and *trust* Him when circumstances don't change as quickly as we want them to.

Our marriage resembled a roller coaster ride as we continued to have "ups" and "downs." Ron was satisfied that he was doing all he could and that would have to be okay. But I knew our marriage was in serious trouble. I had married this man for a relationship and wanted to share my life with him, not just my bed. As the gulf between us widened, I sometimes felt like I was no more than a nanny and maid to him. We viewed marriage from such different perspectives. We were much like witnesses standing on opposite corners observing the same wreck, yet, describing it as if it were two separate wrecks.

My heart was broken over our failing marriage and the dreaded day came when I had to have a complete hysterectomy. When the ultimate realization that I would never have more children hit me, I experienced unexpected, deep grief from this loss. Ron didn't know what to say to make my pain go away. He hoped it would just disappear and I would be happy, again.

My recovery from the surgery was prolonged. Finally, after being bedridden for two months, the doctor discovered a heart condition was preventing my recovery. Now, once again, my health was adding stress to our marriage.

Ron was already overwhelmed with his own struggles and found it unthinkable to add more of mine to his plate. He worked long hours, and I was unable to give him the moral support he needed. So, although together, each of us suffered alone. We were both exhausted and saw no relief in sight.

Then I discovered that this very consistent, stable, dedicated man completely derailed, and the train crash had long-lasting, devastating effects on us all. Ron had gotten off track, and his commitments to his Lord, himself, his family, and his priorities all became distorted.

We all make different choices. And we all disobey God in some area of our life, at one time or another. Your mistakes may be different than Ron's or mine, but the consequences of any sin are the same. They separate us from God's best for our lives, and from fellowship with Him until we ask forgiveness.

I don't know what problems you may be facing today. The details of your struggles may be very different from mine, yet there are similarities in all human suffering and fundamental principles that can be applied to bring restoration. You may be going through the crisis of abandonment, adultery, alcoholism, abuse, drug or pornography addiction, financial disaster, loss of a loved one, a crippling or fatal disease, a jail sentence, or abortion. Whatever shape or form your crisis takes, its devastation affects every life within reach, just like a tornado whipping through a city indiscriminately taking everything in its path. No one lives unto himself – or as the song says, "no man is an island." So, it is when a couple separates or divorces, regardless of the reason. There are many victims, and there are consequences to pay for the choices made, whether they were your choices or decisions forced on you.

We decided to start over, to regroup, to try to put our lives back on track. It wasn't easy. The next two years we merely survived — day by day, minute by minute.

Almost from the moment we decided to start over, Ron threw himself into his work, without even one day of focus on rebuilding our lives. I didn't understand that mindset and was disillusioned.

Now, I understand that this is a common reaction to situations that people don't want to face, or don't know how to handle. We all want to avoid being uncomfortable, feeling inadequate, or experiencing failure. So, Ron spent his time at work where he felt competent and avoided coming home to a situation he just didn't know how to fix.

My interpretation of Ron's actions was that he abandoned our decision to rebuild our lives. I could no longer force myself to believe that things would ever be different, and the pain of my situation was suffocating. No matter how hard I tried, nothing seemed to work; nothing changed. Every waking moment was consumed with thoughts of my impossible situation. Instead of living, I was just surviving. Sometimes my determined will to "make things right" kept me awake for days at a time – my mind furiously analyzing and planning strategies. Then, at other times, I just slept to cope with my grief over my own failing marriage and the reality of the looming negative impact our failures would have on the lives of those in our sphere of influence.

I was in a battle over my physical health and my marriage. And the depression I was experiencing was twofold. The chemical imbalance in my body brought on by the hysterectomy was being addressed by my doctor, but not yet resolved; and, I was suffering from disillusionment over our unchanging relationship. The Bible says in Proverbs 13:12, "Hope deferred makes the heart sick." And, I admittedly felt sick at heart because of the hopelessness of our situation. I became more and more depressed.

With my positive sanguine personality, depression was an unfamiliar emotion to me. I now have real compassion for those experiencing this debilitating state. It's much more complicated than just deciding to "get over it" or "pulling yourself up with your bootstraps." It can be a hollow, dark place where one can quickly get disoriented and lose all hope. This can happen even to a strong Christian. I know. It happened to me.

I simply didn't see how I could get through the day anymore in this condition. I was tired of all of this. Tired of feeling sick, and tired of struggling to bring meaning and life into my marriage. My heart was breaking.

I was going through my private hell, wondering where God was in all this? He was SILENT. It was like standing on a cliff, watching the tumultuous ocean waves beating against the rocks, but hearing nothing. For me, every day, hope ebbed away like the tide, only it didn't return to the shore. It was as if the currents took my hope further out to sea to be lost there, forever.

Once, I remember reaching over to my bedside table to get the bottle of pills my doctor had prescribed for my heart condition. As I poured one into my hand, the thought occurred to me, how easy it would be to end my pain. I watched as the rest of the pills slipped out of the bottle and onto my bed. I moved them around with my fingers, contemplating this dark idea for a moment. Though relief would have been welcomed, thoughts of my children saved me from such an irreconcilable, destructive action. For the first time in my life, I could understand how a person could consider such a thing. These thoughts and feelings were new to me – and frightening. Later I would come to be thankful that God allowed me to experience these thoughts if only momentarily because since that day, I have deep compassion and understanding of how one can get to that point of desperation.

I was not prepared to deal with these painful and unfamiliar circumstances life had thrown in my path. In the beginning, I was determined that with God's help, we could work through our troubles. I would get well; our marriage would survive the trauma, we would stick together, forgive, forget, and move on. After all, God had proven Himself faithful through many trials and tests in the past, and He would do it again. However, I was no longer confident these things would happen.

We limped through the next two years with our marriage continuing to unravel. I pleaded with Ron, one last time to take some time off to focus on mending our broken relationship. It was my last hope to salvage our marriage. He refused.

The usual Scriptures I read didn't seem to work. I could no longer apply Scripture to my life circumstances with confidence. The prayers

I prayed appeared to have no effect at all and to read my Bible no longer gave me strength and comfort. I was numb emotionally. As far as I could tell, God was changing nothing.

These thoughts were new and foreign to me. My faith and my relationship with the Lord had been my anchor and a constant in my life ever since I gave my heart to the Lord as a little girl.

When my mother heard me express my lack of faith, she was shocked. Honestly, I was too. I had never experienced this before. Mother told me she had enough faith for both of us, and she began calling me every day to encourage me and remind me of God's faithfulness. She kept assuring me things would get better. For me, she was like those who held up Moses' arms when he became weary from raising the standard.

My precious mother prayed with me and for me every day. She pointed out to me that she could see improvement, even when I couldn't. It was during this time that I began to realize just how important it is to surround yourself with wise, godly people who not only help you get through the trials of life but guide you when you are vulnerable to making bad choices. Many choices can determine your destiny and the destiny of those around you. Their counsel can protect you from later regrets.

We eventually sought help from counseling to find some way back from our isolated worlds. Ron had little confidence in the counselor and came to a point where he believed it was getting us nowhere. He chose to stop going to the counselor and encouraged me to do so, as well. My parents also tried to get me to stop seeing the counselor as they saw me plummet lower after each visit. My Christian counselor was telling me to divorce; otherwise, I would be setting myself up to be hurt again. My Christian parents were telling me to stay in the marriage. These conflicting messages were disconcerting to me at this incredibly vulnerable time in my life.

I didn't want to believe the counselor's words that Ron would never love me again and that our marriage was irreparable. In Malachi 2:16, God says clearly, "I hate divorce." He loves each of us, but He hates divorce because He knows the trauma and sadness and confusion that it brings to all involved. Why would I want something God hates? I didn't, but at this point, I had lost all hope. I had tried everything I knew, and now this professional was advising me to divorce. At the time, I thought he knew what was best.

It was springtime; fourteen years after we married, but it didn't feel like spring to me. It felt like the dead of winter. Alone and cloistered in my home where we had, in the past, enjoyed many seasons of love and laughter, hopelessness covered me like a heavy blanket. Romance was a distant memory.

Since I was a little girl, life had been simple and straightforward. Now, at my lowest point, I wondered, "How could things have gone so wrong? How did we get to this place?"

The breakup of a family went against everything I believed and stood for. Yet, the dreaded day came when papers were served, and *we separated.* This was the darkest hour of my life – the most painful crisis I had ever faced. Our lives were ruined. Life, as we had known it, would never be the same, again.

When we separated, Ron resigned as pastor. Our church family was very gracious to us. They asked Ron to stay, offering to walk alongside us to help us through this troubled time. We knew, however, that we needed to give our total focus to our family. We were grieved for the confusion we presumed our failure caused them, and for the death of our ministry as we had known it, but we saw no other way.

Now, the questions remained: What would we do? And, where would we go?

Ron and I went our separate ways. It was as if we had come to a fork in the road – he took one, and I took the other, not knowing where either would lead. The children and I packed up and went to my parents' home. They assumed we were going to visit their grandparents, as we had done many times before. So, for them, the trip was a delight; for me, it was gut-wrenching. I knew that with the transition, a very tumultuous time awaited us all. I had a teaching job lined up for the Fall and planned to find a permanent place for the children and me by the time school started.

Ron stayed in town. With no job, he had a lot of time to figure out what was important to him. For him, our separation was a wake-up call. For me, it was the burial of a once beautiful love story.

Ron immediately searched for a new career that would provide the resources to continue meeting our financial obligations. Thankfully, he was able to do so quickly. With that settled, he began pursuing the children and me with a passion. He wanted his family back!

I, on the other hand, couldn't envision how we could ever be a family again. I just wanted to lay aside the ache in my heart and set my life on a new course. I wanted to smile and laugh again — something I hadn't done in a long time.

The children and I flew away for a few weeks of vacation, where I could rest and enjoy a respite from the turmoil surrounding our lives. It was like an oasis in my painful desert that provided much needed emotional relief – even if it was only temporary.

I still had not told the children anything. Our home had not been one of loud arguing and fighting. They were small – just finished first and second grade. Our problems went over their heads, for the most part. A blessing for which I am very grateful. They were not aware of the pending changes in their little lives, and I wasn't ready to deal with their responses to the pending changes about to occur. So, I put off telling them as long as possible. We went on fun outings each day and basically, had an adventurous vacation. The break was good for us. Yet, the days ahead were uncertain.

Chapter Three

The Restoration

L ife, as we had known it, had disintegrated. Could we ever know that life again? Could it ever be restored? We separated. All alone, with nothing else in Ron's life to distract him, he was forced to face the reality of our marital situation for the first time. Up until then, he had wrongly assumed that our lives would always be the same, that the kids and I would always be there. But, when we weren't, he began calling us continually throughout the summer. I was surprised and shocked to hear from him because up until this time, he had given little indication that family relationships were important to him. Other than dispatching his financial obligations, which he did well, his lack of attention, time, and emotional support had been minimal. *But, the possible permanent loss of his family caused his deaf ears to open and his blind eyes to see.* Though neither of us saw it at the time, our separation marked the beginning of our restoration.

Without acknowledging the problem, there can be no change. The crisis of the separation enabled Ron to see our situation from a new perspective. He was finally able to get off the merry-go-round of his horrendous schedule and evaluate what was important to him and what brought us to this awful place. *He eventually realized that a marriage that gets only the leftovers from a busy schedule could die from lack of attention, just like a flower left un-watered.* A relationship must be elevated to a place of value and tended lovingly.

There were many problem areas responsible for our separation that we now know are common challenges to most marriages, and that either one or both of us contaminated our marriage with:

- Wrong priorities
- Forgiveness and repentance, not clearly communicated

- Failure to understand the other's perspective

- Lack of time spent together enjoying and developing an intimate relationship

- Lack of communication that reached the understanding of the other

- Misplaced blame

- Lack of unconditional love

- Guilty of not recognizing that it is God's job to change your mate and your job to love them

- Lack of affirmation and support

- Lack of interest, praising the other's accomplishments

- Failure to acknowledge the other's contributions to the marriage

- A selfish and rebellious spirit

- Failure to convey to your mate that they are needed, cherished and protected

- Refusal to work on the root causes of problem areas

- Lack of spiritual leadership and emphasis on prayer as the glue that holds a family together

- Failure to recognize attempts to please the other or to accept love

- Lack of confidence in decisions

- Unfavorable comparison with others

- Failure to make your mate your priority

- Rejecting your mates' opinions as important; frequently interrupting

- Resentments for past failures

- The inadequate time allowed for preparation of significant life changes

- Lack of a grateful spirit

- Correcting your mate in public, whether with jokes or cutting remarks

- Showing little or no respect for the other in public

When these multiple areas were explored and dealt with one by one, the process of healing, rekindling and the restoration of our love began to take place. Obviously, with so many problem areas to address, the mending of our relationship didn't happen overnight. Even though it was a long and tedious process, *it was well worth the effort.*

These areas caused each of our spirits to be wounded. If there was ever to be reconciliation, we would each have to ask forgiveness and clear our consciences before the Lord and each other. And, we would have to do as Ephesians 5:21 says, "Submit yourselves *to each other* in fear of the Lord." We didn't *want* to do these things, but in time, we ultimately did. It is the opposite of what is humanly natural and culturally acceptable.

Putting his feelings aside, Ron began exploring and trying to deal with each area that had brought ruin to our marriage and endeavored to lead me to do the same. He was convinced that we needed to do whatever was necessary to put our marriage back together.

Nowhere in Scripture does God say it's OK to divorce if you are incompatible, not in love anymore, miserable, not personally fulfilled, or believe it would be better for the children not to have to live in disharmony. God's clear design that once a man and woman have taken vows to stay together until death means just that. The "exception clause," which has its basis in immorality, is the *only grounds* God allows for divorce, and only because of the hardness of men's hearts. It was never His original intention. (Matthew 19:8-9) Staying in the relationship, though not perfect or fulfilling, is ultimately less destructive and has fewer consequences for all concerned than does the ongoing devastation and confusion that divorce brings to all those it touches for generations. If a couple has children, divorce usually only provides some relief and probable lifetime conflicts.

The principles God set up for you to live by are intended for your good. He loves you and wants the best for you. So, based on these Scriptures, outside of an abusive, dangerous, life-threatening situation, it follows that the *best solution*, as difficult and painful as it might be, is to stay in the marriage relationship. Given time, there is the potential for God's miracle-working power to transform it into a loving relationship.

Even if your mate prevents your relationship from becoming what God intended, and you don't get to experience all you want, need and feel you deserve by staying in the marriage, then you move into the arena of what the Bible refers to as, "suffering for righteousness sake." (1 Peter 2:18-3:10) In the latter scenario, while your marriage falls short of your hopes and dreams, you avoid the troublesome consequences of divorce and are in a position to experience many benefits.

Benefits such as:

- Your home remains intact for the children, which provides them with stability and security,

- You set an example for your children that problems are not reasons to destroy a family or forsake a marriage,

- Marriage standards for your children are strengthened

- You keep your children from being subjected to a new and possibly confusing set of authority figures in their lives, which can cause rebellion

- You can develop Godly character in your own life as you depend on God's strength through your difficulties,

- You provide an example for your children and others that reflects Christ's *unconditional love* for His bride, the church.

- Staying in your marriage where God can bring harmony into it is more important to Him than your immediate personal fulfillment. (Ephesians 5:21-33)

If your primary purpose for marriage is for your satisfaction, then you will easily be able to rationalize your way out, and you will not want to hear this "God stuff." You will say that it's all so confusing, yet the Scripture is very clear. What *is* confusing is trying to live God's way *and* your way at the same time. James 1:8 says, "a double-minded man is unstable in all his ways." You cannot go in opposite directions at the same time or consider two opposing thoughts simultaneously. You will eventually decide to play the game of life by God's rules or your own.

If you are a committed Christian whose purpose is to ascertain God's solutions to marital conflicts, you will desire to follow His instructions no matter what you think the cost will be to your fulfillment. You will be able to accept God's ways, and your goal will be to allow Him to build Godly character into your life so that you can influence others for Christ. (Matthew 6:33) Your "suffering" to that end will bring honor to the Lord and certain contentment to your soul. Though you may face daily challenges in your marriage, you will have a sense of inner peace, because you will know you are doing something worthwhile by keeping your children and others from suffering further conflict. God always rewards obedience to His Word. None of this makes sense from a human perspective. You cannot completely understand God's ways, but you *can trust* them. He would never ask you to do anything that would not be good for you.

Our society promotes immediate self-satisfaction and self-fulfillment to such a degree that children are, inadvertently, sacrificed in the process. We are often deceived into believing, sometimes by well-meaning friends, that when our resources of love and patience are depleted, everything will work out and everyone will be better off if we rid ourselves of the one causing us pain. But God delights in proving to a skeptical world the reality and power of His love when our resources are inadequate. (2 Corinthians 12:9; Ephesians 3:16-21)

As Ron considered these things, the more he became convinced that we should reconcile. It was merely a calculated decision to do the right thing, according to Scripture, and expect God to give us the right results. Even though at this point, neither of us had feelings for the other, Ron made numerous attempts over the summer to persuade me of his belief that we should be together. Each time he called, he was met with skepticism and a closed heart. I had shut down emotionally to protect myself from subjection to any further pain. Nevertheless, he very methodically took one step at a time, pressing toward his goal of putting our family back together.

By now, the summer had almost passed, and with our travels completed, the children and I returned to my parents' home. The new school year was about to begin. I would be teaching, and the children and I would be moving into a place of our own, as soon as possible. But Ron had another plan. Instead, he proposed that the children and I move back home, and he would move into an apartment. That way, our children would not have to change schools, and we both agreed that it would be best for them. So, the children and I moved home. I presumed I would rebuild my life there, instead of in my hometown.

Ron's plan to move us back also included putting us nearby so that we would be better able to work on our marriage. However, in my mind, since the separation had marked the *end* of our relationship, I was only moving for the sake of the children, not for Ron and me.

Interestingly, for the first 12 years of our marriage, it seemed like I was the only one working on our relationship. Now, the tables had turned. When I had given up and lost all hope, Ron rose to the occasion. I have noticed that this scenario is not unusual. Ann K. Carroll, a marriage counselor, says in her book, *From the Brink of Divorce*:

> "If you think there's no hope because you are the only one in your relationship who wants or cares enough to try to save your marriage, you are wrong! In my experience, most torn marriages are brought to new

life, new vitality, by the interest, basically, of only one party."

Yes, we all know of marriages that have been unsuccessful. In most cases, one partner gives up when he believes their situation cannot be fixed or that the other partner will *never* change. He cannot imagine living in this condition for the rest of his life. The relationship is suffocating or dangerous. To survive, it seems necessary to get out. Sometimes, one of the mates is unfaithful, and the betrayal causes a grave breach in the relationship. This great chasm often makes the one betrayed develop a root of bitterness toward their mate, sometimes encouraged by others who take up their offense, making reconciliation almost impossible. Perhaps this describes you, or someone you know.

Dr. Ed Wheat, a noted family physician, and therapist makes the following observation in his book, *Love Life For Every Married Couple*:

> "In the great majority of cases, the outcome depends squarely on the committed partner's ability to behave consistently in accord with biblical principles designed by the Author of marriage. So, in a very literal sense, it is *all* up to you. You need not expect your partner to do anything constructive about the marriage if he or she wants out."

Part Two

Lessons Learned

Chapter Four

How to Achieve Restoration

Restoration comes through a commitment to marriage

As you read my story, I encourage you to *never give up.* Even if your mate isn't remotely interested in holding the marriage together, *you can commit to restoring your marriage based on biblical principles and God's promises to you in His Word.* In our case, during our separation, Ron was the first to make a decisive commitment to our marriage and eventually, I followed.

Sometimes things looked grim, and discouragement set in because we could see so little progress, but our hope would grow when we remembered such promises as found in Luke 1:37 which says, "With God, nothing shall be impossible."

Often, we look at the impossible mountains in our lives, and because from the valley, we can't see our way out, and over the mountains, we presume that God can't either. But nothing could be further from the truth. Not only can He see over the mountains, but He can see all the many beautiful things we'll enjoy when we get to the other side. And yes, we *will get there* if we don't allow Satan to deceive us into believing things will never get better.

On those especially challenging days, we relied on Scriptures like Jeremiah 29:11. It says, "I know the plans I have for you, says the Lord. They are plans for good and not evil, to give you a future and a hope." And, one of my favorite Scriptures, Romans 8:28, "God causes all things to work together for good to those who love God, to those who are called according to His purpose." These promises gave us the courage to try one more time.

You must be willing to be committed for the long haul purposefully working to improve your situation every single day. The restoration of your marriage must become of paramount importance to you, and you must commit to doing whatever is necessary for however long is needed to get what you want. Don't quit too soon. If it took you ten years to get your marriage all messed up, if necessary, give it that long to get it all fixed up! It will be hard. There will be days when you feel you have taken three steps forward and two steps back, but at least, there will be some progress and evidence of change. Keep on keepin' on!

Should you decide to make this kind of commitment to your marriage, pray that God will turn your mate's heart toward reconciliation, and trust Him to bring about a fantastic future for the two of you to share. Be patient. Be very patient. Remember, restoration usually begins with the commitment of one, and usually takes a very long time. In our case, this was certainly true.

We were married for twelve years, separated for six months, experienced about eighteen months of intense struggle as we worked through issue after issue, and spent another couple of years continuing in the process of maturing before we felt comfortable and confident in our relationship. We've now been married over four decades, and we're still discovering new ways to deepen the rekindled love and respect we have for each other. I'm so grateful Ron made the conscious commitment to reclaim our marriage and family. It has made all the difference.

Restoration comes through reclaiming the marriage relationship

Reclaiming a relationship doesn't just happen. First, you deliberately decide that is what you want, then go after it with intentionality. You must "name it before you can claim it." Olympic champions don't just stumble into winning the gold medal. They decide what they want, evaluate what it will take to get what they want, formulate a plan, and deliberately pursue the plan. You can do no less if you're going to reclaim your marriage and experience success in this area of your life. You don't have to just *hope* it will happen. You can take steps to *make* it happen.

Ron did just that. He decisively took charge of putting his family back together. Then, he was a committee of one who began the process of reclaiming his family, alone. His first and major task was to get us all back in the same town. With this accomplished, he began instigating the rest of his plan to reunite us, which primarily included spending as much time as possible with the children and me and endeavoring to *show his intentions of being a devoted husband and father.* Since I had lost all hope, I was not responsive to his efforts, at first. I still felt numb and dead inside.

I was, however, glad to be back in my own home that we had built two years before and where we intended to raise our children. The house where we planned to mark their growth on the pantry door frame. I had picked out every detail down to the doorknobs. And here, our children's dog had two litters of puppies in a homemade box tucked in the corner of our breakfast room. These walls contained many fond and precious memories along with many sad ones for Ron and me. Part of Ron's plan to reclaim his family centered around replacing these painful memories for the two of us and continuing to make happy memories with the family.

Restoration Place

In the first 12-years of our marriage, we moved nine times. We both were ready to put down roots when we built our home. Part of Ron's plan to reunite us included getting us all back in the same town and making the house we had built together a *place of restoration.* We had carefully built it to accommodate a growing family where the love of Christ was proclaimed and evident in all that was said and done, and he sought to re-establish that original intent. He, also, made efforts to cooperate with my heart's desire to make our home a warm and inviting place where friends and family were welcome. He purposed to remove the turmoil and restore our home to a place of peace and harmony.

I had taught school before the children were born. Then, I devoted my energies and attention to be a full-time mom, to hospitality, and ministry. I was dedicated to my roles of wife and mother, as well as pastor's wife. These roles suited me perfectly. So, being away for the summer had been quite difficult, not just because of the house, but all that it represented to me. Somehow, being back home and close to the familiar things offered a measure of comfort. Ron was wise to put us in a place where restoration could most easily occur, though I was not thinking in those terms, at that time.

The children and I got settled back home just in time for them to start school. This year our children would be second and third graders. I started back to work, a very deliberate step toward becoming self-supporting, self-sufficient, and independent from Ron. I dropped the children at a friend's house just before daylight since my work was so far away. She took them to school for me. Another friend picked them up and kept them until I returned from my long day at the office. By the time I got them home, it was already dark outside. I fed them, put them to bed, and started all over the next day.

Ron began his new career to support himself and reorder his life. In the evenings, he would sometimes come over and participate in tucking the children into bed so he could see them. I had long before established a nighttime routine of telling them stories, giving them hugs and kisses, and talking with them while rubbing their little backs.

Taking a tip from the bedtime ritual for the children, Ron started offering to give me back rubs, as well. I was so exhausted from the day of work; I found a back rub next to impossible to resist. And, as unassuming as it may seem, I believe this simple act of "touching" became a significant point of physical contact and a step in re-establishing a connection between us. At the time, it was the only kind of tenderness I was able to receive from Ron. Years before, I had learned the value of properly touching your children and teenagers as a point of contact—thus, the bedtime back rubs. But I had no idea that it would be one of the tools that would subtly reconnect Ron and me.

Though my office job was great, I was miserable being away from my children so much. There just wasn't enough time and energy left at the end of the day to work on developing their character, to shape their values, to train them spiritually, or even give attention to teaching them polite manners. I had no time to think about establishing a new identity or future for myself, either. This was not what I visualized my life to be.

In his book, *"What Wives Wish Their Husbands Knew about Women,"* Dr. James Dobson says,

> "There are few women alive who are equipped with the super strength necessary at the end of a workday to meet the emotional needs of their children, to train and guide and discipline, to build self-esteem, to teach the true values of life, and beyond all that, to maintain a healthy marital relationship, as well. Perhaps the task can be accomplished for a week or a month, or even a season, but for years on end? I simply don't believe it. To the contrary, I have observed that exhausted wives and mothers become irritable, grouchy, and frustrated, setting the stage for conflict within the home."

I was not alone in my fatigue and frustration.

As we began to circulate in the community again, I was embarrassed about our failures and concerned about those we had disappointed. I was devastated over the loss of our testimony and ministry, and now, over the loss of personal identity, as was Ron. He was no longer the pastor of an exciting, visionary church, nor I the pastor's wife in charge of the women's ministry.

Though we both felt like utter misfits, we did, at least, share that commonality, and oddly, it drew us together. We were in the same city. The children and I were at home, and Ron was over often making great efforts to be positively involved in our lives. He was feeling good about his idea of bringing us together to the same place where restoration could more likely occur.

Restoration of identity and worth

Several months later, I was invited to attend an event for ladies at a nearby church. The speaker's topic was "Our Identity in Christ." I don't remember much about the evening. I can't tell you what the speaker looked like, or even her name. But I can tell you that God performed healing in me that night through her words and the Scriptures she boldly proclaimed. As tears flowed down my face, God burned the truth into my mind that I belong to Him. I am a child of the King of Kings!

I don't have to perform up to what I perceive are His expectations or work to gain His love. When I fail, He still loves me and accepts me, just as I am. That night, He bathed me in His unconditional love, and I realized my identity as *His child* was all the identity I needed. I don't have to have a job or a certain kind of car or home, or even human relationships to define who I am. My relationship with Him gives me a special place of service and value. That night, God graciously restored my lost identity.

Chapter Five

Restoration through Elevating Marriage and Family

On a practical level, Ron began *showing* me how important it was to him for the family to have a primary place of importance in his life. He was giving us his best time and trying to be sensitive to our needs. According to Scripture, our relationship with God should come first, then our mate, our children, followed by church and career. For Ron to do this was a major departure from what I had known of him, and though giving his family priority was precisely what I longed for, I was concerned that it wouldn't last. It would be a long time before I could find it in my heart to completely trust him. But I could see evidence that he was trying to restore the family to its proper place of priority, and his efforts were beginning to warm my heart.

It's challenging for men to spend time with their families because their job of providing for them is typically demanding. While physical provision is admirable, a wife and children have other needs, as well, and can't wait until retirement to have those needs met. There is only a small window of opportunity to establish a special relationship with a child, and that window sets the stage for a lifetime of pleasure or regret. Children pass through our homes so briefly. The influence and guidance of a father are of chief importance to their development and stability, as is his attention to his wife.

A key to healthy family relationships, for a father, is found in balancing the scriptural admonition to *provide,* to *lead,* and to *love.* It's complicated to achieve, but oh how necessary it is. For a husband and father to have his priorities in line with Scripture makes all the difference in his life and the life of his family.

Scripture instructs fathers to:

Provide: "If anyone does not provide for his own, and especially for those of his household, he has denied the faith and is worse than an unbeliever." (1 Timothy 5:8)

Lead: "Fathers, do not exasperate your children; instead, bring them up in the training and instruction of the Lord." (Ephesians 6:4)

Love: "Husbands, love your wives, just as Christ loved the church and gave himself up for her." (Ephesians 5:25) "Husbands, love your wives and do not be harsh with them." (Colossians 3:19)

It's difficult to balance these three commands, but in Luke 12:31, God provides a way: "He will always give you all you need from day to day if you make the Kingdom of God your primary concern."

Simply put, when a man lives according to God's plan, God promises to take care of him, his family, his business, and all that concerns him. In other words, when a father puts God first, God promises to align everything else in his life.

Sometimes when Ron and I are tempted to take control of our circumstances, and "logic our way through," we remember a principle we both learned as children and attempt to continue applying it now that we are married. It's a financial principle that can be applied to other areas of life. It's the principle of "tithing," that is, giving the first ten percent of your earnings to the Lord. When we married, we were not making quite enough to cover our monthly bills, but we were obedient to tithe, anyway, giving that first ten percent of our meager monthly earnings to the church. Miraculously, every month, we came out in the black. For example, people gave us food that stretched our groceries, and an odd job that provided the little extra income we needed. God's math is different from ours, but it sure works! And this principle also works when applying it to prioritizing our time, and other areas.

Chapter Six

Restoration Through Wise Counsel

T*hose you surround yourself with in times of crisis will dramatically affect your life decisions.*

Since our separation, we had not seen a counselor nor were either of us eager to do so. But a former pastor of mine, who was aware of our circumstances, set us up with a Christian counselor. He was confident this man would lead us closer to reconciliation, to which I was beginning to be open. However, based on our previous experience with a couple of Christian counselors who had not prayed with us or brought godly principles into the counseling room, we were very reticent to seek the help of another counselor of any kind. In retrospect, we both felt they had done more harm than good. We ultimately agreed to see this man, and he proved to be very helpful, indeed. We were thankful we gave counseling another try. He brought God into the healing process and taught us to practically apply biblical truths that began to bring a ray of light into this dark place in our lives.

He helped us with communication skills, encouraging the use of words of affirmation, appreciation, affection, and kindness. He aided us in blaming less and building up each other more. These communication skills sound so basic. And, while we often use them on others outside of our home, we are sometimes guilty of forgetting the importance of using them on the people we love most. He also explained that though we are "opposites," as most couples are, we could learn to view this as a great asset. We would have to operate as a team, put our strengths together and learn to *appreciate these differences*, rather than allow them to be a source of conflict. Since men and women were created to serve different purposes, they are wired differently to be able to accomplish those specific tasks; thus, they will always view life from opposite perspectives. That fact will never change. So, it's best to *accept* it and learn to make it work *for* you.

We were making progress as we endeavored to apply these concepts, but it was slow, very slow. My precious family learned of a well-respected marriage workshop and paid for us to go. They strongly believed in "marriage for life" and very much wanted to see us together and happy. They hoped this workshop would escalate our progress. I appreciated their concern and their generous offer, but I was afraid… afraid that even if we went back together, things would return to the way they had been before.

Not wanting to get trapped or be a temporary project, I declined to go. Ron didn't know if it would be beneficial either, but agreed to try it, and ultimately, I succumbed to their pleas, as well.

We boarded a plane and very hesitantly walked into the workshop the next morning, as did, probably, every other couple there. Uncomfortable is perhaps a good way to describe the general atmosphere. But, very quickly, the workshop facilitators helped us all to turn our focus on our purpose for being there. There was no mistake, their intent and goal for each of us was reconciliation.

They encouraged us to remove the words "separation" or "divorce" from our vocabulary and out of the realm of possibility for our relationship. They said this would help us clarify our life direction and enable us to put our total concentration on rebuilding without wasting energy on deciding if we would start over again. We began to realize that if we allowed ourselves a back door to get out of the relationship, we were in constant turmoil. The indecision drained us of valuable energy that we could have otherwise use toward making our relationship work.

Ron had apologized to me long before coming to the workshop, but it was there that he finally communicated a repentant heart for the turmoil he brought into the relationship. He appealed to me to be open to the idea of going back together and promised that this time, we would pattern our marriage after God's design. At this point, I was able to become vulnerable to him and crack open the door of my heart, once more.

He said we just needed to *do the right thing to get the right results* and God would take care of the rest. In other words, Ron believed if we would go back together and follow God's prescription for a successful marriage, and begin to act like a couple in love, that eventually, we would be in love. After feeling rejected and ignored for so long, I found the idea of being loved and "in love" very appealing.

During the workshop, I realized I needed to make some changes, too. I needed to be less critical and perfectionistic in my expectations for our relationship, and let God be the one to change Ron and me. I also needed to take responsibility for my lack of faith that God could transform our marriage, no matter how serious the infractions, and for the consequences of my responses that caused us to be apart.

Both of us needed to forgive each other and focus on the good that God could bring out of this trauma. We needed to trust God to, someday, *turn our mess into a message.*

I can't say we fell back in love at the marriage workshop. We didn't. It took a long time. But, before we left at the end of that week to return home, we did decide to end the six-month separation. We didn't base our decision on our feelings, but instead on what we believed the Scripture implored us to do. We seriously considered the consequences of the never-ending conflicts of divorce versus the possibility that our family could be restored and our love rekindled. Oh, we knew it would never be perfect, but it was undoubtedly the best of the alternatives.

Upon our arrival home, Ron left his apartment and moved back in with the children and me. It was awkward for us, at first, because we were acting out of obedience, not out of love. *We had to learn to proclaim that which wasn't as if it were.* In other words, we had to talk to each other as if we were in love and act in ways that would show that we were in love before we were in love. This is *unnatural!* It's walking "by faith."

When you have been hurt, betrayed, misunderstood, or the brunt of a myriad of other offenses, one of the hardest things in the world to do is treat the person responsible with kindness. While it is tough, it's also powerful, and it works!

In Matthew 5:44, Jesus said, *"Love your enemies! Pray for those who persecute you."* So, even if you perceive your spouse to be your enemy, you are to love them. Since this is not a normal human response, we must rely on the One who can do it through us, remembering the promise, *"I can do all things through Christ who strengthens me."* (Philippians 4:13) We must trust God to help us behave in loving ways, especially if we believe the other person doesn't deserve it. Eventually good feelings, that we are unable to muster on our own, will appear.

Chapter Seven

Restoration of Spiritual Relationships

First and foremost, Ron and I both realized we needed to get our personal spiritual lives back on track. Through the long, fiery trials in our relationship, when God didn't move in *our* timetable, we became impatient and began relying more heavily on human reasoning than on insights from the Bible for direction. We had both become spiritually dry. For us to experience God's blessings, we had to start making decisions that would bring us closer to God, and we began that process by attending church together, again.

We no longer had a church home since we didn't think it was appropriate to return to the church that Ron had pastored, so we just started visiting other churches. It was uncomfortable for both of us. Though it was agonizing for Ron to sit in a pew instead of stand behind the pulpit, I admired the fact that he took the initiative to bring us and was grateful for this show of spiritual leadership for our family. I saw it as a first step in reuniting us spiritually, and the exposure to worship gradually brought a renewed spiritual awakening in our hearts.

We realized our root sin of taking control of our own lives, rather than trusting God. We had to surrender our will to His and submit our rights and expectations, correct prideful attitudes, conditional love, and negative feelings toward the other. I knew God loved Ron, so when I was unable to love him, I had to ask God to love him through me, and Ron did the same. While all of this can be said neatly and concisely, it took months to work through each of these issues and to see some small amount of growth in our spiritual maturity.

Over time, as we depended more on Scripture and on the power of prayer to bring about desired changes in our lives, our faith began to grow, and God began to work. We confessed each sin to the Lord, one by one, as He brought them to our minds. And, as we each grew closer to God, we also grew closer to each other.

Restoration through right priorities

We began the slow, arduous process of rebuilding our marriage the right way – God's way. This time, God (not to be confused with the church) would have priority in our lives, then our marriage relationship, then the children, and then church and career. And this time, we would strive to follow more closely the directions for a healthy marriage so clearly mapped out in the Bible.

Restoration through godly living

To ensure a healthy marriage, we tried to follow the guidelines in 1 Peter 3:1-16 and 1 Peter 4:8-11, making them our model:

> ". . . wives be submissive to your husbands so that even if any of them are disobedient to the word, they may be won without a word by the behavior of their wives, as they observe your chaste and respectful behavior. And let not your adornment be merely external-braiding the hair, and wearing gold jewelry, or putting on dresses; But let it be the hidden person of the heart, with the imperishable quality of a gentle and quiet spirit, which is precious in the sight of God.

> You husbands, likewise, live with your wives in an understanding way, as with a weaker vessel, since she is a woman; and grant her honor as a fellow heir of the grace of life, so that your prayers may not be hindered. To sum up, let all be harmonious, sympathetic, brotherly, kindhearted, and humble in spirit; Not returning evil for evil, or insult for insult, but giving a blessing instead; for you were called for the very purpose that you might inherit a blessing.

> For let him who means to love life and see good days refrain his tongue from evil and his lips from speaking guile. And let him turn away from evil and do good; Let him seek peace and pursue it.

For the eyes of the Lord are upon the righteous, and his ears attend to their prayer, but the face of the Lord is against those who do evil. Sanctify Christ as Lord in your hearts Keep a good conscience."

"Above all, keep fervent in your love for one another, because love covers a multitude of sins. Be hospitable to one another without complaint, as each one has received a special gift, employ it in serving one another, as good stewards of the manifold grace of God.

Whoever speaks, let him speak, as it were, the utterances of God; whoever serves, let him do so as by the strength which God supplies; so that in all things God may be glorified through Jesus Christ, to whom belongs the glory and dominion forever and ever."

Ron and I also tried to be faithful to Deuteronomy 6:7 by making our home a sanctuary where we could fulfill the following admonition:

"You shall teach them, (my commandments), diligently to your children, and shall talk of them when you sit in your house and when you walk by the way and when you lie down and when you rise up."

This training at home was in addition to what they learned at church. *We did not allow anything other than our personal relationship with God to come before our family.* We would not let "the good to rob us of the best."

Ron led us in family devotions, and we also endeavored to teach our children to have their own private time with the Lord. Finally, *prayer had a significant place in our home,* once again.

Restoration through focusing our thoughts on good things

Though we had a perfect model to follow, we were far from perfect and old habits were hard to break. The major breaches that had come into our marriage took time to heal and rebuild. At times, I became discouraged and wondered if things would ever really be different. I remember telling my mother one day, that I could hardly see any progress because where we were was so far from where we should be. But she was always there to encourage me and assure me that our circumstances were, indeed, much improved. I could depend on Mother to be my cheerleader in every situation, pointing out to me positive things she was able to observe. For instance, she noted that not only were Ron and I back together, but we were beginning to function in more unity. We were spending more time together, and even occasionally laughing together.

Mother reminded me of the good things in my marriage I could focus on, even though we had a long way to go. It was just what I needed to help me keep on trying another day. The Bible says in Philippians 4:8-9 to: *"Fix your thoughts on what is true and good and right. Think about things that are pure and lovely, and dwell on the fine, good things in others. Think about all the things for which you can be grateful... and the God of peace will be with you."*

At one point, Ron and I made a list of the character qualities and other things that had attracted us when we first started dating and that ultimately brought us together in marriage. We kept this list in a place we could refer to many times throughout the day so we could read it over and over, saturating our minds with good thoughts toward the other. We have recommended this activity to many couples as it can be strengthening to any relationship, at any stage. Learning to *refocus our thoughts* was just one of many baby steps we took on our journey toward a healthy marriage.

Restoration through communication and conflict resolution

It's important to realize that every action and every word spoken either contributes or contaminates a relationship.

I needed to *hear* Ron express his affection and communicate to me the desires of his heart if I was going to be able to respond to him. I was weary of trying to read his mind or second-guess what his intentions were. Ron began expressing himself by writing letters. At this point in our relationship, it was easier for him to put his feelings on paper than to say them to me face to face. He was a beautiful writer, and after a while, his words began to penetrate my heart.

In addition to the letters, and his willingness to be more verbally communicative, he also communicated his desires in his behavior. He began courting me. He asked me out on dates where the purpose was to make new pleasant memories. We spent that time together talking only about good things – giving some relief to working through issues with me and courting me. He brought gifts and sent flowers. After a while, there were too many to keep in the house, so I planted them outside where I could see them from my kitchen window. Those flowers bloomed every year for over 20 years! Let me say, in my yard, that's a miracle! The flowers were a continual reminder to me of how important it is to work through tough times and to trust God's faithfulness in trials and tests. There's something very gratifying that only comes to the depth of your being after working through difficult circumstances, rather than quitting.

It had been difficult to appreciate the nice things Ron had done to strengthen our relationship because he still refused to discuss the foundational issues that brought our marriage to crisis and separation. Being relegated to talking only of pleasantries was, to me, like building a house and trying to put up the walls before the foundation was in place or applying wallpaper before the walls were up.

In the months that followed, as we kept things on a surface level, life was pleasant. He wanted to "move on" which was good, but not without discussion that would lead to "fixing root problems" that led to our crisis in the first place, and would again, if not addressed. Communication on this deeper level was necessary to me so that issues from the past would not surface to haunt us in the future.

Restoration through persistence

Anger and distrust lived in the place where love used to reside.

Even so, Ron persisted in his efforts to show kindness, and I tried to do likewise. Persistence in "doing the right thing, over and over, to get the right results" meant that before we felt like showing kindness, we did it anyway. Our cold, stone-like hearts eventually softened. And when we wanted to blame the other for the downward spiral our lives had taken, we had to persistently forgive each other.

Forgiveness isn't something you do one time; it's something you do persistently. Aristotle said once that *we are what we repeatedly do.* We consistently tried to find at least one specific, positive thing we could do each day to improve our relationship, no matter how small it might be. A smile, a kind word or action, a note. And we focused on the things that *we could* control. *I could not* control Ron, for none of us can or should try to control another person, but *I could* control myself. *I could* choose to fellowship only with people who would encourage me toward our goal of rekindling our love. *I could* choose to control my thoughts, allowing myself to entertain only positive thoughts toward Ron. *I could* manage my schedule to enable me to bring balance into my life. Together, *we could* continually strive to get to know each other in depth, so that we could understand, love, help, and encourage each other, and meet each other's needs.

We both learned to *do different things to get different results.* We persistently acted, talked, and responded differently to situations and this changed the paradigm of our relationship, opening it to new possibilities. Ron, for example, persisted in attending all the school functions, and endeavored to be involved in each of our lives to a greater degree than in the past. And, he persisted in trying to make everything as easy as possible on us by seeing that the car was in good repair, and the yard maintained. He supported us financially so I could again be a full-time mom. I hadn't seen Ron pursue his family with the same kind of passion he had pursued the ministry. His persistence in all these areas spoke volumes to me about where his heart was, and this was one more step in bringing us closer. Was God transforming my husband into a new man?

I persisted to learn to develop new methods of communicating with one another so we could solve the real issues plaguing our relationship. Ron knew that I was no longer willing to accept surface-level communication. This would also require a lot of time that we were unaccustomed to spending together, so we had to persistently allocate our time differently. We also had to be persistent in building a strong foundation that would stand the test of time where our family had its right place of priority.

Perhaps the most important element of persistence in our restoration was that we decided not to give up on our relationship. We consistently looked for ways to strengthen it, and on days when the other didn't respond as we might hope they would, we made a commitment to keep trying. *We purposed not to look at where we were, but to visualize where we could be.* Dr. Frank Minirth, Christian Psychiatrist says, "Persistence is a strong, strong factor in reaching your potential."

Let me encourage you to be persistent for you to realize your dreams and goals. It's been said, "it is darkest just before morning." After having suffered long in a disappointing relationship, I fear many have missed the sunrise in their life and marriage by not persisting just a little longer.

Restoration through improving your health

Ron began reading books on marriage. I had never known him to do that before. They awakened him to some insights into husband/wife relationships he had not previously known. One book was very helpful. It was written by a Christian Psychologist, Dr. James Dobson entitled, *"What Wives Wish Their Husbands Knew About Women."* Among other things, it provided the answer to a chemical imbalance in my body that had puzzled my doctors for two years. That discovery revolutionized my life!

My earlier hysterectomy had eliminated the disease that previously caused pain during our most intimate times, and thus relieved the problems in that area of our life, but it brought on the severe hormone imbalance that further aggravated my heart and thyroid condition.

Because of this, the doctors had not been able to properly regulate my system. This put me in a constant state of extreme fatigue along with varying degrees of depression. No doubt, my medical condition severely impacted my ability to concentrate and cope with the logistics of a cross-country move and the stress in our marriage.

Through the information in Dr. Dobson's book, Ron discovered that in rare cases, hormone replacement given by mouth is simply not assimilated into the body. After discussing this idea with the doctor, tests were made and later revealed that though I was taking a very high hormone dosage by mouth, it was as if I was not taking any medication at all! So, I was then given the medication by injection, and immediately took a dramatic turn for the better.

Health issues can dramatically affect relationships, so it's important to resolve, as far as possible, any that may negatively affect your relationship. Do everything you can to approach life with a healthy body. Even adding a simple exercise program to your schedule during times of stress can be beneficial to your physical health, as well as your mental health. When our counselor suggested exercise for this reason, I remember thinking that I couldn't possibly do that. I didn't feel like it. I didn't have the energy to exercise. I already felt overwhelmed and didn't see how I could add anything else to my day. But, I did, and I was surprised that it made such a difference. If nothing else, it helped me to think about something besides my problems. I later came to realize that *replacing problematic thinking with positive thoughts is a significant step in the healing process.*

Many doctors believe that during exercise, the body produces more endorphins and enkephalins, chemicals, which help relieve pain and promote a feeling of well-being. Scientists say these chemicals control the brain's perception of, and response to pain and stress. It is also probable that laughter produces these same chemicals. Perhaps that's why the Scripture says, "A joyful heart is good medicine." (Proverbs 17:22)

During difficult times, it's common for the problem stressors to consume our every thought. Soon, the whole world seems full of trouble. We start feeling down and depressed and life appears to be full of one unsolvable problem after another. Exercise and laughter are wonderful ways to input something positive into our lives during the difficult, stormy days, enabling us to deal with life more effectively.

Restoration through Obedience

Because of Ron's obedience to Scripture to guide us in a godly direction by rebuilding our marriage, in spite of our feelings to the contrary, our marriage and my health were restored. When Ron stumbled across the answer to my health problem while reading to find ways to strengthen our relationship, I believe that was God's way of throwing in one of those "abundantly above what we could ask or think" blessings. *God honors obedience!*

Restoration through the Influence of Godly People

Ron and I were beginning to realize the significance of being surrounded with people who could help us focus on the good that remained in our relationship rather than on the bad. My family and most of my friends helped me focus on godly principles that would bring us back together. Ron also had those in his life who encouraged reconciliation. Looking back, I am amazed at the powerful influence these people had over this very vulnerable time, and how their counsel drastically affected the outcome of our lives.

We all like it when someone pulls to our side in support, but when they are offended on our behalf, or take up our offense, they often oppose a reconciliation. We both had this occur, as well. In their effort to be helpful, these people impeded the probability of our marriage being salvaged. And, even when we were willing to reconcile, they remained offended and encouraged us, by their attitude, to do the same. Independently of each other, Ron and I both came to a point where we realized we had to separate ourselves from anyone, be it counselor, friend, co-worker, or relative, who influenced us in this way. While they were well-meaning, we believed they were giving us counsel that was opposed to Scripture. So, we needed to wisely choose who we would spend time with and take advice from, for our lives to go in the direction that we wanted.

One of the most important principles of reconciliation we learned was to *be careful who you surround yourself with in times of crisis.* Filtering all advice through the light of Scripture was vital to the survival of our marriage.

Restoration through Encouragement

Many years ago, my husband and I took a five-day, whitewater rafting trip down the Salmon River in Idaho. It was fun and exciting! It was certainly an unfamiliar experience for a city girl who was sure the picture of the lodge, with indoor "facilities," had been accidentally omitted from the brochure. They couldn't really be serious about sleeping in tents for five nights! This river is called the *River of No Return*, because travelers once could not navigate against is furious current and rapids. It was on this tumultuous, unforgiving river that I learned the importance of a "take charge, confident guide."

On the third day, we were a little nervous, because our guide had warned us we would be navigating through dangerous waters where, previously, some had lost their lives. We started down river in our raft with my husband just ahead of us in a small kayak. Suddenly, he was thrown out of it and was being helplessly tossed by the roaring waters. Our guide, who had been calmly calling out instructions to our rafting team up to that point, instantly realized the danger my husband was in and kicked into high gear. He knew exactly what needed to be done and though he was concerned, was not as emotionally involved as the rest of us who knew Ron. With great authority, he yelled out over the rushing waters swift instructions to my husband and to the eight of us in the raft. When the first few tries to save Ron failed, the guide rallied our best efforts for one last attempt. His urgent plea, confident plan, and explanation of the consequences if we didn't rescue Ron this time caused us to work furiously together as a team to get the desired result. And we did! Ron was saved! I can assure you; I could not have accomplished that rescue on my own. **It took a team** and a confident guide.

Marriages that are racing downriver being dashed against the rocks and taken under by the currents need rescuing, too. So, I implore you, go to those who are navigating in tumultuous waters, alone. They may be worn out. They may have given up. Don't let them be taken by the *River of No Return* because of Satan's deceptions. Go to them again and again until you have snatched them from the crashing, violent waters that would bring death to their marriage. Be their team and direct them to the Lord's guidance.

Ron and I are grateful for the team of people in our lives who loved us enough to come alongside each of us to lend their support and guidance. Each one can take credit for the valuable role they played in bringing us together. Some sent letters or called, some brought resources such as books, others listened or gave advice, some shared biblical counsel, and some made it financially possible for us to go to marriage workshops, and most all of them prayed fervently in our behalf. Most of the time, they were tender, but when we had a bad case of "stinkin' thinkin'," as the late Zig Ziglar said, it was necessary for them to be tough to cause us to refocus and get back on track.

Perhaps right now, you are thinking of someone who needs a cheerleader or an encourager. We so often hesitate to step into peoples' lives for fear of interfering or offending them, but I appeal to you for those who are unwilling or unable to ask for themselves, do it anyway! People in pain don't always know what they need. They are depleted of energy and usually believe they have tried everything known to man to solve their problems, so no one else could possibly have an answer either. Whether they recognize it or not, they need a caring person with a clear head who is not emotionally involved, and armed with biblical principles, to be their undaunted guide through this tumultuous time.

Some would say this forward approach is not very realistic. That we shouldn't meddle in other peoples' affairs and, besides, we're all so busy with our own lives. My answer is, I'm glad Jesus doesn't offer one invitation to come to Him. He gently keeps coming back, time after time, until we are receptive and open our hearts to Him. If the Lord is prompting you to be that someone for a friend, obey! You will be blessed and so will they.

If you are the one in trauma and no one has come to you, you don't have to suffer alone. It's OK to seek out a friend or counselor and tell them what you need, as best you can. They may genuinely care, yet not believe themselves adequate to help you. There is a way out of your pain – don't stop until you find it!

Restoration Summary

Looking back, it hardly seems right that only a couple of years of struggling with failure out of a lifetime of faithfulness, could change our lives, forever. But it did.

During this dark time in our lives, I didn't see *how* any good could come from all the pain and suffering. But now, I know from my own life experience the reality of the scriptural principle that when bad things come into our lives, it is God's design to bring good from them.

Satan's plan was to ruin our ministry, our marriage, our children, and future generations, while God's plan was to make us stronger through our suffering and develop in us His character. It was to take the ashes of our lives and turn them into something beautiful through His restorative power.

I would like to tell you that within a few weeks or months, that our marriage was healthy and strong. But I can't honestly do that. For us, after ending our separation and deciding to rebuild our marriage, it took about five or six months to repair the feelings of rejection and begin to fall in love again. Then, it took several years to rebuild the trust, to learn effective communication, and remove the root causes of our problems. I have no doubt that God has the power to heal relationships in a moment, and perhaps sometimes, He does. But, most of the time, it involves a *process of healing* over time. Psychologists tell us when there has been a serious breach in a marriage, the couple should expect to spend the next two to five years working on their relationship before enjoying a strong marriage. Ron and I are still discovering new and exciting ways to improve our relationship.

Our own experience bears out the truth that the healing of a broken marriage involves a *gradual process* built on *multiple choices* that determine our destiny. I didn't just wake up one morning, look at Ron and "feel" love for him. It was more like, I realized I didn't mind doing his laundry so much anymore, or I wasn't as angry with him as often, or the idea of our being a family wasn't so painful but, possibly even a good thing. Constant thoughts of our tragic marriage no longer consumed my mind, in fact, they were beginning to be replaced with happy thoughts. It gave me pleasure to see him interacting with the children, and the sounds of laughter were again heard in our home. We planned fun dates where we decided not to talk about anything in the past or "work on our relationship." Gradually, we began to enjoy each other. I remember the first time I laughed in Ron's presence. I was surprised because I thought I would never smile again. It was just over a simple thing.

The Bible says in Proverbs 13:12, "Hope deferred makes the heart sick, but a longing fulfilled is a tree of life."

And in Proverbs 17:22, it says: "A merry heart doeth good like a medicine."

I realized with this newfound joy, that hope had returned, and we were getting well. We seldom speak of that difficult time of our lives. We've been too busy having fun, enjoying the family, and dreaming together about our future. Just last night, we laughed together, wondering what we'd look like when we're 90!

The healing comes through:

- *The process of forgiving.* Forgiving our mate over and over and over again – even when they don't deserve it and even though we have already forgiven that particular offense many times.

- *The process of focusing.* Focusing our thoughts on the good throughout the day until it becomes a habit.

- *The process of good choices.* Making choices throughout the day that determine whether there will be harmony or hurt, healing or havoc in our lives.

We make many choices over a lifetime. It's important to give those choices intentional thought with a plan of action to carry them out. *Choices can powerfully affect our restoration.* Some choices move us away from our goal of restoration, and some lead us to it. The following choices make restoration possible:

Choose always to do the right thing

To give your marriage another try, whether you "feel" like it or not, is an example of "doing the right thing to get the right results." There were many such instances that I did what people do when they're in love, even though I certainly wasn't in love.

One of those occasions was on the first Valentine's Day after Ron and I went back together following our separation. I still had no feelings for him. Remember, we had come back together only because we had made a commitment to be obedient to God's plan for marriage, and to take the word "divorce" out of our vocabulary. Things were only creeping toward improvement, and at this point, and I was discouraged. I certainly didn't want to give him a mushy valentine! But I went to the store, anyway, to do what couples do who are in love – buy a Valentine card. Nothing seemed to do. They were all about love and warm, fuzzy feeling. But I was persistent and finally found one that was rather bland. After all, I was obligated to keep my commitment to "do the right thing to get the right result," but I didn't want to be a total hypocrite!

Choose to obey God's Word

Neither Ron nor I *wanted* to rebuild our marriage, but we had a great appreciation for God's holiness and His Word. We knew we must obey. We read in Malachi 2:16 that God hates divorce. Based on nothing but Scripture, I realized, that we could not improve on God's plan. That even with the exception clause regarding adultery, God's best plan is to restore. You don't have to automatically opt out for that reason.

Choose to trust God

He knows what is best for us. Just like a loving parent always answers their child's plea. God always answers the pleas of His children. Sometimes He answers "no," sometimes "wait," and sometimes "yes." Our part is to trust our sovereign God who loves us deeply, and just as we want our children to understand that because we love them deeply, we can be trusted to do what's best for them, even if we say "no" to them.

When we do our part, God will keep His promises and do His part. And therein lies the MIRACLE that cannot be explained in human terms. I cannot tell you how God accomplishes this, but I *know* He does! He did it for us and He can do it for you. The Bible tells us that He is no respecter of persons, so what He has done for our marriage, He can do for yours.

A little chorus I learned as a child still serves me well. It goes like this:

> "Got any rivers you think are uncrossable?
>
> Got any mountains, you can't tunnel through?
>
> God specializes in things thought impossible, and
>
> He can do what no other power can do!"

(By Oscar G. Eliason, © Universal Music Publishing Group, Capitol Christian Music Group)

Choose to pray

Prayer changes things. The answer may not come when we want it. In fact, it probably won't. God's timetable is nothing like ours. The Bible says that to God, a day is as a thousand years, and to us, it surely does seem that way when we are waiting for Him to answer our prayers.

I have waited over 40 years for some of my prayers to be answered. But I assure you, in each case, it was worth the wait! Most people are not willing to wait on God. They give him a little time, then they say, "I can't take it anymore." But what they are really saying is, "God didn't answer quickly enough, I'll just do it myself."

When God told Abraham's wife, Sarah, that she would bear a child in her old age, she laughed. She couldn't imagine how this could possibly happen, so after a time, she took matters into her own hands. She came up with the idea that she would have her handmaiden sleep with her husband, a common practice in that day, thus giving her a baby in her old age. This turned out very badly. She created a mess because she was impatient, and she didn't trust God to do something miraculous in her life. However, in God's timing, Sarah did become pregnant and had a child in her old age, just as God promised. All good things came as a result.

Many of us are like Sarah. But I implore you to *be uncommon*. Wait on God. Believe me…

> "HE IS ABLE to [carry out His purpose and] do superabundantly more than all that we dare ask or think [infinitely beyond our greatest prayers, hope, or dreams], according to His power that is at work within us." Ephesians 3:20, Amplified Bible

On the other hand, sometimes God answers quickly. The point is, God answers in what He knows to be the perfect timing for all involved. You can trust him.

Choose to end well

When we come to the end of life, we all want to hear God say, "Well done, thou good and faithful servant." *We want to hear Him say*, "You trusted me, and at personal sacrifice, you allowed me to work in your life. As a result, I accomplished my purposes for you and those around you, and, ultimately, brought you great joy. You were a good example to the world of my sacrificial, unconditional love, of how important forgiveness is in relationship, and your marriage reflected the love I have for my bride, my people. I am proud of you."

We don't want Him to say, "You were impatient, you didn't trust me, you were selfish and cared more about your own happiness. Your pursuit of personal fulfillment robbed your children of security and caused them untold emotional pain. And, your decisions caused those in your sphere of influence to stumble, to lower their standards, to doubt my Word and that I could do great and mighty things in their lives. I'm disappointed in you."

Chapter Eight

15 Keys to Reestablish and Rekindle Relationships

There are many keys involved in reconciling a relationship to be able to enjoy a rekindled love. Some are listed below:

1. Forgiveness is a choice – it is a gift you give your mate

2. Forgiveness is also a process

3. Discover and address root causes of problems – don't just treat symptoms of the problem

4. Decide to be better, not bitter

5. Decide to do it God's way, not your own

6. Do the right things to get the right results

7. Important to surround yourself during this vulnerable time with wise, godly people who will give you biblical counsel

8. God is the healer

9. Choose to love again – Yes, you can love again through His strength.

10. Visualize your mate the way God sees them and ask God to help you love them that way.

11. Focus on solutions rather than on problems

12. Seek biblical counseling

13. Focus on what you have left, not on what you've lost

14. Meditate on the Scriptures that can bring healing to your life and be an encouragement to you.

15. Read the Bible and books that will give you hope. "Streams in the Desert" by Mrs. Charles E. Cowman is one of several devotional books that brought hope to my soul when I had none.

Chapter Nine

Promises from the Word and Songs for the Heart

O ne of the things that got me through this difficult time in my life was a small frame containing five Scriptures that I placed beside my kitchen sink. I read them over and over, hundreds of times, often with tears streaming down my face, and thought about the power in those words. They brought healing to my mind and soul.

- "He heals the brokenhearted and binds up their wounds." Psalm 147:3

- "He hath sent me to... comfort all that mourn... to give unto them beauty for ashes, the oil of joy for mourning, the garment of praise for the spirit of heaviness" Isaiah 61:1-3

- "My grace is sufficient for thee: for my strength is made perfect in weakness" 2 Corinthians 12:9

- "Let Him have all your worries and cares, for He is always thinking about you and watching everything that concerns you." 1 Peter 5:7

- "Behold, I will do a new thing: now it shall spring forth... I will make a way in the wilderness, and rivers in the desert." Isaiah 43:19

The last Scripture was given to me by my mother. It was such a profound encouragement that I wrote a chorus based on the verse as a praise to God and with the desire to bring hope to others:

"I am intimately acquainted with thee.

Not one tear is wasted with me.

I will make a way for thee.

Even in the desert places I'll be.

I am the God of new beginnings, you see.

At this difficult time, put your trust only in me."

During those days, I was so troubled, I could only get through the day by focusing on the next minute.

When you get discouraged, let the lyrics to this little song I wrote encourage you:

You are there

"When everything around me starts to crumble,

And I can't make any sense of it at all,

When stripped of who I am and ever hoped to be,

You are there and on your name I call.

You are there, You are there.

Every time I call your name, you are there.

And you are all I need.

When darkness, doubts, and confusion overwhelm me.

I can feel your holy presence and your love.

Your right-hand lays hold on me to guide me,

I will not fear.

You are there and on your name I call."

He is faithful to be there when you need Him, and He is sufficient to meet every need you may have. He is the God of a second chance. He's ready to give you peace, hope and assurance. Assurance that when we follow God's formula for marriage and family relationships, we are sure to experience success and blessings.

Chapter Ten

Encouraging Others

Don't hesitate to walk with another through a valley of hopelessness. They need you to guide them gently to the mountaintop. They are tired of the battle and vulnerable to doubts Satan and, perhaps, well-meaning, but misinformed friends, bring to their mind.

You may feel unqualified to help another because you have struggled yourself. However, someone has said, "Our most important messages grow out of our greatest weaknesses." Be transparent. Be real. You will be surprised at the healing your support brings into their life.

You may be weary from your own life battles. But having gone through them and successfully come out on the other side, you have stories to tell, a testimony to share, that could be encouraging to one still in the battle.

Chuck Swindoll says: "History proves that struggles and scars pave the way for remarkable achievements." You, and the one you are encouraging, are on a path to great things. God uses greatly those who have suffered greatly. Gloria and Bill Gaither in their song, "I Will Serve Thee", expressed it well when they wrote,

> Heartaches, broken people
>
> Ruined Lives are why He died on Calvary.
>
> Your touch in what I long for...
>
> You have given Life to me.

Chapter Eleven

Restoration of Ruins

My friend, my prayer for you is that the reading of our story has birthed in you a new trust in God to heal your broken heart and your shattered dreams.

Ours is a testimony of how God restored our marriage.

We once thought our lives were ruined; now our love is rekindled. Our family is restored, and life is rich with abundant blessings. Where I was once concerned that our children would grow up to be casualties of the ministry, instead they grew up in a stable, Christian home where their father was a guiding influence and force in their lives. God answered my prayer of many years that our family would be a Christlike example to others. As he so often does, He answered in a very different way than I imagined He would. My vision was only that we would model a healthy Christian family. God's vision included that, plus life lessons on forgiveness, and God's restorative power to transform lives and families. We are still learning and growing and by no means a perfect example, but God has transformed our marriage and led us on a journey from the deceptions of Satan into the light of God's truth.

Our children are now grown. God has rewarded us for obeying His commands to keep our family together. They have not grown up rebellious, but rather each loves the Lord with all their heart. Our son has a master's degree from the seminary in Counseling. And, our daughter has a doctorate in theology. They both have a heart for ministry.

Where I used to see Ron as my opponent, I now see him as *my champion.* He is an attentive, devoted husband who makes me feel cherished. His strong leadership and aggressive nature enable him to be an outstanding provider and a tender father whose children adore him. Our son regularly seeks his father's wise counsel, and, I've heard our daughter express gratitude that her daddy always has time for her – even in the middle of a critically important meeting. He is a man passionately devoted to his family. I will forever be grateful to Ron for centering our family on the foundation of God's Word.

God changed me, as well. He taught me that in the dark, unfamiliar places of life where it's easy to lose my way, to lose hope, to give up, that He is always there to guide and comfort me. And *He really is all I need*. While I may *feel* utterly alone and deserted, I most definitely am not. If I have other people in my life who love and appreciate me, that is a bonus, but in actuality, He will supply my every need – He promised. When I feel overwhelmed, He wants me to cast my cares on Him and trust Him with each one because He can be trusted completely. And even when things don't make sense, and I cannot "see" His hand at work in my life and circumstances, I know He *is* working and very much in control. He grew my faith and taught me that nothing is too hard for Him. And, He takes pleasure in answering my prayers, though not always the way I imagined, or in the timing I preferred, but He does answer.

All my life, I heard the Scripture, "I can do all things through Christ who strengthens me," Philippians 4:13. But, I didn't know until I went through this shattering experience that my love for someone could turn to hate and that "all" meant forgiving and learning to love someone who had hurt me so deeply. I could never muster up enough strength on my own to accomplish such a task. I think I realized, perhaps, for the first time, how much I needed the power of Christ at work in me.

Perhaps, some of the lessons I learned through this season of my life that are most precious to me are:

I am special because of my identity as His child, and no one can take that away!

No matter how badly I "mess up," He can still use me, and bless me, and love me with an everlasting love.

I genuinely believe that if I had not been willing to forgive and trust, again, that the end of this story would be very different. We would have had continual conflict, financial troubles, angry and rebellious teenagers, and a split home, which would have been a poor example for our children to follow. I don't believe they would have surrendered their lives to serve the Lord in their chosen professions as they have.

God restored our home that is now a haven for all of us from a hurried world where we try to share God's love and grace with all who enter. Our home, now, is often full of family and friends, one of God's best gifts. God not only restored our marriage, but He also put a desire in our hearts to walk alongside couples whose marriage is struggling, and to strengthen other families through teaching and counseling.

God took the very thing that was our greatest weakness and has used it to help others.

He transforms our mistakes and failures into miracles - making out of them something useful and meaningful if we are willing to let him.

Ron and I are still growing and deepening our relationship, and I hope we never stop. We continue to reorder our priorities, putting each other in the proper place. We have learned how to make our differences work for us, rather than against us. And now, we realize our extremely opposite gifts and abilities make us a strong team. We keep discovering new things to appreciate in each other.

Like all marriages, we still make mistakes. But we've learned to accept and offer forgiveness to one another quickly. And, we've learned to accept each other as we are, love each other unconditionally, and put the other first.

When Ron and I decided to start over, he arranged for us to have a marriage ceremony in which we *renewed* our vows. The same pastor that ordained him to preach, many years prior, performed the ceremony, and his precious wife stood as our one and only witness. She took a picture to commemorate our decision, and Ron gave me a rose. This simple little ceremony stood in contrast to our large beautiful wedding fourteen years earlier. This day, the celebrating crowd in the sanctuary consisted of only the four of us, and we were not in love. It was nothing more than an act of obedience to God and His Word. In time, part of God's reward was to rekindle and strengthen the love for each other that we had lost.

Our experience taught us that love is not a feeling; it is a decision to "Do the right thing to get the right result." Often the most difficult decisions are made alone or with few to stand with us. With God on our side, that's a majority! We're so thankful to God for the victory He gave us that day and for continuing to grow our faith. Ron and I believe that a healthy marriage is a gift from God and part of the heritage we are now able to leave to our children and grandchildren.

Once, I thought my life would never be the same, again. I was right. It isn't the same. It's BETTER! Ruined – No! Rekindled – Yes!

We, with our own making,

RUINED our **LIVES**, but God

REKINDLED our **LOVE,** and

RESTORED our **MARRIAGE**.

Praise be to Him, forever!

Chapter Twelve

Commitment to Marriage

Choose to commit to building your life and your marriage God's way.

What is His way?

1. Right relationships with God, your mate, and others. Ask forgiveness. Seek to restore fellowship with anyone you have wronged. God is so serious about this; He says it is the only way He will hear your prayers. Scripture references include 1 Peter 3:7, Mark 11:25-26, Matthew 5:23-24.

2. Live by His principles.

3. Get into the Word.

4. Take "divorce" out of your vocabulary. God hates divorce so why would you want something He hates?

5. Read the Song of Solomon as a marriage model.

6. Commit that anything that will lead you away from God's best for your marriage will not be a part of your life.

7. Don't let good rob you of the best.

8. Eliminate the poison of pornography from affecting your relationship.

9. Prioritize your time and relationships: God, family, and career.

10. Touch affectionately.

11. Pray and play together.

12. Trust God to guide decisions and choices that affect your relationship.

13. Believe God has a magnificent plan and purpose for your marriage and ask him to help you achieve it.

14. Leave the past in the past. To focus on your rearview mirror while driving is to head for a collision.

15. Be patient. Remember that God *usually* works through process, not overnight miracles.

Let me offer an illustration:

I was driving to work, using the same route I had taken for months. Each day, I glanced at a dead looking field on my left, and day after day, it looked the same, brown and dead. Spring came, and I continued to take the same route. But, one day, when I passed the field, it was covered in the most beautiful array of wildflowers I had ever seen! It took my breath away!

As I thought about it, I realized God works in the same way. We can't see the work he is doing "underground" in the winter seasons of our life. We sometimes wonder if He's forgotten all about us and our million requests to bring about change in our lives. But, finally, one day, things do change! Finally, Springtime comes into our life, and we can see what God had been doing in the winter months of our life.

We really can trust Him to honor our commitments to follow His commands and principles for marriage or life in general. He's always up to something GOOD on our behalf.

Consider asking your pastor to conduct a private session for you and your spouse to renew your wedding vows.

Chapter Thirteen

The Foundation of Godly Marriage

In December 1967, the evening news made a startling announcement. South African surgeon, a preacher's son, Dr. Christiaan Barnard had performed the world's first heart transplant. He had placed the heart of Denise Darvall, a woman in her mid-twenties, who was fatally injured in an automobile accident, inside the chest of fifty-five-year-old diabetic, Louis Washansky, who had incurable heart disease. Louis' new heart was actually beating on its own. That was amazing!

When an interviewer asked Dr. Barnard why he had decided to perform such a risky operation, his answer was, "One look at Mr. Washansky, and I knew he couldn't live with that old heart."

The basis for success in life, including success in marriage, is the proper foundation. A godly marriage involves three: a husband, a wife and God. We are told several times in Scripture of our need to be born again. When both a husband and his wife are committed to the lordship of Christ, they are in sync. Neither is demanding his, or her, own will. Each is surrendered to the will of God. They honor Him by honoring each other.

There is a tension in every marriage because there is tension in *every* relationship. In fact, there is even a tension in our relationship with God. God is perfect and holy, and we are not. Unlike marriage, this is a tension we do not have the ability to resolve. No matter what we do, God's anger toward our sin cannot be fixed. Since, we could not provide a way forward, God did it for us. He breached the divide between His holiness and our sinfulness by sending His Son.

Jesus was God and man and lived a sinless life. As a perfect person, His death on the cross meant something significant. He was without sin, so all the guilt for all the sin we committed could be placed on Him. We sin. He was sinless. We are guilty and he was punished. In this way there was an exchange. We receive his mercy and grace: He received the punishment for our sin. The innocent is treated as guilty so that the guilty could be treated as innocent.

To prove this was all true, Jesus rose from the dead. This testified to His claim to be the Son of God and gave us great hope! After all, if He rose from the dead, He could raise us to life one day.

However, knowing the truth of God's love toward us is only the first step. We must act on what we know. Jesus called this action, this reception of God's plan for us, a new birth.

If you have never experienced the life-changing experience of the new birth, why not now? Turn your life over to the Lordship of Christ and invite Him into your heart to forgive your sin and to live His life in your heart. Either of you can experience God's salvation and new life; or both of you together. Here is the path.

1. Recognize and admit that you've sinned against God.

2. Acknowledge that you need a Savior, that you cannot save yourself.

3. Repent, by turning from your sins.

4. Believe in your heart that Jesus died on the cross, in your place, to pay for your sins.

5. Believe in your heart that the Father raised Him from the dead on the third day. He is alive!

6. Trust Jesus Christ as your personal Lord and Savior by inviting Him to come into your heart, forgive your sins, cleanse you from sin, and live His life through you.

Are you ready? Good.

Right now, right where you are, turn to God and say,

Dear God, I know that I am a sinner and I've sinned against you.
I need your forgiveness. I need a clean heart.
I am turning from my sins. Forgive and cleanse me. I trust you as my Savior and give my life to you. Come into my heart today, Risen Christ, and be Lord of my life. I choose to follow you. Thank you for the new life you've given me. Thank you for my new, clean heart. In Jesus' name I pray. Amen.

Did you sincerely turn to Christ? Did you invite Him into your life? Then congratulations! He has washed away your sins and now lives in you! This is what the Scripture calls *being born again,* a supernatural work of God's Spirit, who is now within you.

This is the only cure for spiritual heart trouble. Now, with Jesus as your Savior and with your new heart, you have eternal life! Now you can relate to Him on a brand-new level. He is your Father, and you are His child. Best of all, when you take your last breath here, you'll be in His presence.

Here are some suggestions to help you develop and deepen your new relationship with God.

1. Get to know the Lord by reading your Bible every day. I suggest you start with the New Testament book of Philippians.

2. Converse with God continually through prayer. Talk with Him. He is your Father. Tell Him how you feel and what you need.

3. Don't allow sins to pile up and rob you of your joy. Make a practice of confessing your sins on a daily basis.

4. Above all, listen to Him. He will speak to your heart through His Spirit.

5. Attend a Bible-teaching church where you can worship and serve God and fellowship with other believers.

6. Ask the pastor to baptize you, as Jesus has commanded each of us. Water baptism is a symbol of the fact that you've put off

your old life in sin and have put on your new life in Christ. It's a testimony to others that you are now a child of God.

7. Share your new life with others. Invite them to do as you have done so they too can experience God's peace and live forever with Him.

Chapter 14

Final Thoughts

Decisions that Determine our Destiny

Every decision we make leads us in one direction or another. Each decision can lead us a step away from God's plan, or a step closer to His plan. His plan is good for us. So now you must decide, will I start taking the steps in the right direction? Let me say it more strongly: you must start taking steps. Will my marriage be restored? Well, I can't tell you that, but I can tell you this, you will not get there if you don't start walking in the right direction and making wise decisions!

Here's the truth few people will tell you: Most often marriages are not restored with one big conference, book, or break through. Rather restored relationships are the result of a collection of good decisions over time. Like any achievement, a collection of right choices together achieves the goal. Ready? OK. Here we go.

1. Find a wise counselor

We learned through our counseling experiences, the importance of wisely choosing a counselor. With the same care you would use to select a surgeon to whom you would put your life into their hands in the operating room, you should select a counselor. If you are seeking a Christian counselor, it's important to ask questions such as:

Do you use biblical principles in counseling and to what extent? If not, what method do you use?

Is prayer a regular part of your counseling sessions? Explain.

With our specific set of circumstances, what would be your ultimate goal for the sessions?

Example: Under what circumstances, if any, would you ever recommend divorce?

What made you decide to go into counseling as a profession?

Have you ever been under the guidance of a counselor? If so, were you pleased with the way you were counseled and with the final result? What method did they use?

Are you happy with the way your life has turned out and where you are at this point?

These are just some sample questions. The idea is to be sure that this person will ultimately lead you in the direction *you* want your life to go. It's good to evaluate the "fruit" of any person's life from whom you are receiving counsel. Not that they have never made mistakes, but did they learn from them and is their life working now, and are they presently living under God's blessings? Another way to put it: Don't ask a lost person for directions. Do ask a champion how to win.

Maintain an attitude of gratitude

We had to decide what kind of *attitude* we would have. And, it *is* a *decision*. When we look for things that we can be grateful for, it lifts our spirit and corrects our negative attitude.

We found it essential to continually ignore feelings that produced negative attitudes toward each other. *Feelings are deceptive and irrelevant when it comes to making right choices.*

I remember when my son was about four years old, and I was teaching him to say he was sorry to his sister. He was a real little thinker. I will never forget how he put his hands on his hips and said, "Mommy, if you make me say I'm sorry, you'll be making me lie." At first, he almost stumped me! Then I replied, "No son, I'm not making you lie; I'm making you 'say' the right thing." Often, when we say the right thing, the desired feelings follow.

2. Follow the Scriptural admonition to be thankful

"In everything give thanks: for this is the will of God in Christ Jesus concerning you." 1 Thessalonians 5:18

It's hard to be thankful when your life is falling apart. That's when faith comes in. God knows that if we can thank him, not for the tragedy itself, but for the good things that He will bring from it, our trust in Him will increase, and we will be positioned to be open to new experiences, and able to move forward in our lives.

3. Be happy regardless of your circumstances

Dr. Frank Minirth, a Christian Psychologist and author of multiple books on relationships, declares that laughter is healing, and happiness is a state of mind we can decide to have.

4. Keep on keeping on

Don't quit when life gets hard. The late Dr. Robert Schuller says,

"Tough times never last... but tough people do," and

"When faced with a mountain *I will not quit!* I will keep on striving until I climb over, find a pass through, tunnel underneath-or simply stay and turn the mountain into a *gold mine*, with *God's help!*"

5. Love again

Our destiny is determined by the things on which we set our minds. Permit yourself to fall in love again. Yes, you may get hurt, but you may not! Set your mind on your goal and then take the risk!

6. Trust God to heal your soul

God knows you're hurting, and He promises to give you, His precious child:

"Beauty for ashes, the oil of joy for mourning, the garment of praise for the spirit of heaviness." Isaiah 61:3

7. Believe that God can bring good from your painful and disappointing circumstances

"All things work together for good for those who love God, to those who are called according to His purpose." Romans 8:28

8. Be kind

Being kind to those who are kind to you is easy. We don't need anybody to tell us to do that. However, God tells us to be kind, even to our enemy, which would include that mate who has hurt you. He says, "Love your enemies, bless them that curse you, do good to them that hate you, and pray for them which despitefully use you, and persecute you…" Matthew 5:44

It's near impossible to hate someone you're praying for and someone for whom you're looking for ways to be kind. We are empowered when we allow the spirit of God to act through us in these ways. And, the heart of the enemy is eventually softened, making a change in the relationship a possibility.

9. Remove the word "divorce" from your vocabulary

Decide divorce is not an option to consider when things get tough. Without this "back door," you will be more resolved to find a way through the difficult times.

Appendix

Friends and Enemies

One of the reasons marriages fail is that there is not enough fighting! Every marriage has enemies. In order to win we must play offense and beat the enemy! Remember your spouse is not the enemy. So, we must fight, but fight *the right* enemy. Below is a simple list of Marriage Builders, and another list of Enemies of Marriage.

Marriage Builders

- Defer your desires and rights

- Honor your mate

- Affirm your mate

- Look for the things that drew you to your mate in the first place

- Compliment your mate on the character qualities you observe in them

- Love unconditionally

- Lower your expectations. Expectations get us in trouble. Sometimes we put unrealistic expectations on our mate that God himself couldn't achieve. Don't expect your mate to meet all your needs. That's too much to expect from anyone and a heavy burden for another to carry.

- Find your identity in Christ, not in your mate

- Work together to formulate a mission statement for your marriage

- Talk the same language. You cannot read each other's mind anymore that you can understand a foreign language you never learned. Read Gary Chapman's book entitled, "The Five Love Languages." It will help you learn how to communicate with your spouse the way you best receive love, and how he best receives love from you.

- Pray together

- Worship together

- Laugh together

- Go on dates. Restore your marriage through romance

- Turn off the TV, put your cell phone away, get off your computer, and *talk*

- Make memories together

- Build a life together – *Dream* together

- Work on a project together – something you both feel passionate about

- Realize that *separation* is not a trial to see if you still love each other after being apart – it is a serious step in the direction of a divorce.

- When you separate, you begin a series of steps that develop a mindset of independence from your mate: physically, emotionally, financially.

- Separation takes you in the opposite direction of building a relationship. So, outside of a dangerous or abusive situation, separation is not recommended if you truly want to move in the direction of strengthening your marriage.

- Learn to accept others, accept yourself, and accept your circumstances. Acceptance is the first step toward contentment. It takes away the urgency for change and allows time for God to move in His way. "Be" content in all ways.

- Be thankful

- Don't be anxious, trust instead that things will get better.

- Choose not to be easily offended

- Remember that it's "Not how far you fall, but how fast you get up" that matters

- Replace negative thoughts and talk with positive ones. "Whatsoever things are true, whatsoever things are pure, whatsoever things are lovely, whatsoever things are of good report; if there be any virtue, and if there be any praise, think on these things" (Philippians 4:8).

- Listen to worship praise music

- See yourself not as *being under your circumstances*, but victoriously *rising above them*

- Get a health checkup. Make sure you're operating at your best level of health, so you, in turn, will have the energy for the work required to maximize your marriage

- Exercise. It releases endorphins that help level out emotions

- You can fall back in love

- Smile. You really can be happy, again!

- Be a peacemaker

- Get your finances in check. Doing so will remove stress for you and your marriage.

- Realize there is *hope* for the hurting

- Balance your life. Manage it, don't let it manage you.

- Develop a sense of purpose

Enemies of the Home

Be alert and sensitive to the following enemies that cause the destruction of home and marriage relationships

- Conditional love

- Wrong priorities

- Discontent

- Unbelief

- Unforgiveness

- Failure to give up your rights

- Criticism

- A disorganized, unkempt home where chaos prevails

- Technology: TV, Phones, Tablets and Computers

- Workaholism

- Perfectionism

- Pornography

- Failure to spend time together. We all want to be with a person who makes time for us, who makes us feel good, and who makes us feel special.

God is Faithful

- Remember, God is faithful. He hears your prayers and answers.

- God knows your name. He knows where you are. He knows what you're going through. So, "Give all your worries and cares to God, for He cares about you" (1 Peter 5:7).

- He is Sufficient to meet your every need. 2 Corinthians 12:9 says, "My grace is sufficient for you, for my power is made perfect in weakness."

- He's *all* you need.

- You can make it! Yes, you may feel like you're the *only one* working on your marriage. Dr. Ed Wheat, in his best-selling book, "How to Save Your Marriage Alone," discusses biblical concepts that can transform a marriage when only one person is applying the principles of building a loving relationship consistently.

- "With God nothing {is or ever] shall be impossible," (Luke 1:37).

- Your problems are not too big for God. He will finish what He began in you. It's not too late. Do not fear. Never, never, ever give up!

Tribute to My Wife Kay

Ron Cherry

I met Kay when we were in the fourth grade. During my senior year of high school, we fell in love. We dated throughout college and married while in graduate school. On December 18, 2020 we would have been married for forty-eight years. I say this to tell you that I have known this woman all my life. There has never been a day in my adult life that I did not think of her, nor have I made any decision during that time that did not take her into consideration. No one has a better knowledge of her than I.

Kay had great credentials! Miss Teenage Beaumont, graduate of Louisiana State University in New Orleans, elementary teacher, speaker, singer, summa cum laude graduate of the Criswell College with a master's degree, mentor to dozens of young women, pastor's wife and too many other things to list. Her real credentials were the many people to whom she ministered and whom she loved, and they are countless.

Kay was all about Jesus and people. She loved both in the extreme. When with her, she made you feel as though you had known her forever, and she probably said something encouraging to you before the conversation ended. She was a genuinely happy person and that made her a wonderful mate. She forgave my shortcomings and praised my victories with equal sincerity. Only her love for the Lord rivaled the love she had for her family. She deeply loved her five grandchildren and would have had us all together all the time if she could.

Marriage to Kay was a privilege. My grief is that her absence has come too soon. My only consolation is that I will see her in heaven with the Lord she loved.

"To be absent from this body is to be present with the Lord."

2 Corinthians 5:8

Tribute to my Mother

Jason Cherry

Relationships are one of the fundamentals in life. One's relationships to God, spouse, family and friends require an enormous amount of time and effort. Of those relationships, marriage is one of the most significant that we experience. My mom understood that, and much of her life was devoted to improving relationships. I admire her for always pursuing a right relationship with those she loved.

In this book, you will find real life stories of struggle and pain, but also encounter stories of overcoming hardships in life and attaining peace, joy, and satisfaction in and through relationships. As a former marriage and family counselor, I have read many books on this subject, and my mom's book stands out! You will be drawn into the vivid stories and learn important lessons along the way.

I am so grateful that my mom and dad elevated their relationship with each other and God intentionally, even when it wasn't the easy choice. You will find great value in this book and will want to share it with others.

Thanks, Mom, for leaving us with so much wisdom!

I pray that through this book, Kay Cherry may have as great an impact on you and your family relationships as she has in our family.

Tribute to my Mother

Ashley Cherry Smith

When I was six years old, I remember quietly peering around my mother's bathroom door. I was watching her put on makeup. She saw me and allowed me to quietly observe her. I wanted to be just like this beautiful, gracious lady. Now, I am grown with three children of my own and I still want to be just like my mom! My mother was a great beauty, but her heart was truly golden. She was a woman of strength, integrity, honor, love and peace. She believed the truth, spoke the truth, and lived by the truth of God's Word.

In addition to being mother and daughter, we were also best friends. So, I know intimately about the struggles and hardships she faced in life. There are not enough pages to describe my love and respect for her. One of the reasons I respect my parents so much is their herculean effort to salvage a ruined marriage. Not only did they attempt something great (upholding God's design for marriage), but they accomplished something powerfully Divine. Their marriage modeled the supernatural mystery described in Ephesians Chapter 5. Despite nearly every valid excuse to divorce, they chose instead to obey God and believe He could make a miracle out of their mess. My parents purposed to live for a reason beyond themselves and show the world how great the love of Christ is for His Bride. They died to their own desires, hopes, and needs so they could sacrifice for one another, for their children, and for all who looked to them for guidance.

Instead of being a child plagued by the brokenness of divorce, I was allowed to watch God at work and given the privilege of being a witness to the work Christ came to earth to accomplish – healing, redemption, restoration and resurrection! Throughout life, we are offered many opportunities to see and understand the gospel. Jesus came to earth as the Divine Holy One to live a sinless life and die on our behalf to soothe the wrath of God. His sacrificial death provided salvation for any who would call on His name for salvation and forgiveness. After His shameful and painful death, Jesus was buried until three days later when He rose from the grave. All who are united with Him have the promise of resurrection and eternity with Him in heaven.

My parents taught me these truths and they lived the truth before me. Their marriage, which was designed to display the love of God, fell ruined and broken, battered and bruised. It seemed beyond repair. But their obedience led to living sacrifice. God resurrected their love to make a great good-news story. I had a front row seat for this transformation! Because of their example, I also carry the burden and challenge to model this mystery in marriage in my own life.

It was so sweet to watch my parents in their last years together! They overcame, they dreamed, laughed, served and loved together. Writing this book was very important to my mother. She wanted everyone who struggled with marriage to find the same restoration that she and my Dad found because they chose obedience to God over everything else. My parents are a great inspiration to me, and I hope they will be to you as well!